Writing Contemporary Topics in 15 Units

文法・用法もよくわかる
トピック英作文 **15**章

by Haruo Kizuka

TSURUMI SHOTEN

画像クレジット

Unit 1 ©SeanPavonePhoto–fotolia.com
Unit 2 ©ladysoulphoto–fotolia.com
Unit 6 ©liza5450–fotolia.com
Unit 7 ©milatas–fotolia.com
Unit 9 ©and4me–fotolia.com
Unit 10 ©ISAS/JAXA
Unit 11 ©sv650ksr80–fotolia.com
Unit 12 ©Paylessimages–fotolia.com
Unit 13 ©ivychuang1101–fotolia.com
Unit 14 ©JensHN–fotolia.com
Unit 15 ©kawa10–fotolia.com

はじめに

　日常のニュースや友人との会話などに出てくる話題で「こんなことを英語で書けたり話せたらいいなあ」あるいは「英語では何というのかな」と思うことがよくあることと思います。本書はそうした現代の日本で関心を持たれている話題を素材にして、その話題に関する文や会話を適切な英語で表現できる力を養うことを目的として編まれています。

　本書の特長は、各ユニットで最初に文法の重要事項や日本人の間違いやすい英語の用法などを復習し、次に英作文の問題練習をするようになっていることです。基本的な単語の学習や慣用表現の確認もできるように配慮してあります。

　以下、簡単に各ユニットの構成を紹介します。

- 冒頭コラム：各ユニットへの導入部として日本語で書かれたコラム。
- **Dialogue**：ディクテーションにもなっている冒頭コラムに関連した対話。
- 文法上の注意：前述の会話文中の文法上の注意事項の説明。
- 用法上の注意：同様に会話文中の間違いやすい用法の説明。
- 慣用表現：覚えておくべき慣用表現とその使い方の例文。
- **Exercises**：
  A：各ユニットのトピックに関連した単語問題。
  B：文法的、用法的に正しい方の語句を選ぶ2択問題。
  C：ユニットの冒頭コラムと関連づけした英作文問題。
- **Supplementary Exercise**（巻末）：コロケーション問題。

「読む、書く、話す、聞く」のいわゆる英語の4技能のうち、「書く」技能を磨くことが一番地道な努力を必要とするかもしれません。このテキストが学生の皆さんのそうした努力の一助となることを切に願っています。

　最後に、本テキストの作成に当たり、すべての英文に目を通してくださった早稲田大学名誉教授 James M. Vardaman 氏、およびいろいろ助言をしていただいた音羽書房鶴見書店の山口隆史社長に心からお礼を申し上げます。

2016年秋

　　　　　　　　　　　　　　　　　　　　　　　　　　　　　　木塚　晴夫

CONTENTS

UNIT

1. Flourishing International Tourism 1
   盛んになる国際観光
2. Increasing Popularity of Japanese Food Abroad 6
   海外で高まる日本食の人気
3. Homestay 11
   ホームステイ
4. The Olympic Games and the Paralympic Games 16
   オリンピックとパラリンピック大会
5. The Nobel Prize 21
   ノーベル賞
6. Keeping in Shape 26
   健康維持
7. Job Hunting 31
   就職活動
8. University Reform 36
   大学改革
9. Merits & Demerits of Smartphones 41
   スマートフォンの利点と欠点
10. Japan's Feat of Space Science 46
    日本の宇宙科学の快挙
11. Japan's Food Self-sufficiency Rate 51
    日本の食料自給率
12. A Low Birthrate and an Aging Society 56
    低い出生率と老齢化社会
13. Global Warming 61
    地球温暖化
14. A Widening Gap Between Rich and Poor 66
    拡大する貧富の格差
15. Bad Manners 71
    マナーの悪さ

    Collocation Exercises 76

UNIT 1
Flourishing International Tourism

盛んになる国際観光

旅ほど楽しいものはないと言われており、人々は豊かになると国内は勿論海外へも旅行するようになる。2015 年には 1621 万人の日本人が海外へ行き、日本を訪れた外国人は前年より 47 パーセント増え 1973 万 7 千人にも達した。国際観光は異国の文化や人々をよりよく知るばかりか、ビジネスの活性化にも役立つので、日本政府は日本へ来る外国人を更に増やすため、空港や宿泊設備の充実や観光ビザ発給の条件緩和などさまざまな政策を講じている。政府はオリンピックが開かれる 2020 年には日本を訪れる人が 4 千万人を超えることを期待している。

‖Warm-up‖

次の会話を聴いて空欄を埋めなさい。

Dialogue

A: (   ) is just around the corner. Do you have any plans?

B: Yes, **an American friend of mine** and I are planning to go to California. (   ) and brought up in San Francisco and is going to show me around his native state.

A: How nice! When I was a college senior I studied in New York (   ), and on my way home I **stopped over** in San Francisco. I made a sightseeing **tour** of the city and also went to Berkeley, where the University of California is located.

B: Did you? (   ) you enjoyed the brief stay in the Bay Area.

A: Yes, I did, but I missed a chance to visit Yosemite National Park. I didn't have time because I had to finish my graduation thesis as soon as I returned home.

B: (   ). Everyone says Yosemite National Park is **worth visiting** because of its breathtaking natural beauty, and it's the place in California **which** I'd like to visit most of all.

Notes:
 native「出生地の、故郷の」／ **state**「州」／ **senior**「4年生」／ **make a sightseeing tour**「観光する」／ **on one's way home**「帰途」／ **be located**「〜に位置する、〜にある」／ **Yosemite National Park**「ヨセミテ国立公園」／ **the Bay Area**「ベイエリア（サンフランシスコ湾岸の地域）」／ **graduation thesis**「卒業論文」／ **breathtaking natural beauty**「息を呑むほどの自然美」

文法上の注意

❏ an American friend of mine と my American friend の違い

 前者は「アメリカ人の友人」で特定の人を指していないのに対し、後者は「たった1人のアメリカ人の友人」か「特定のアメリカ人の友人」を指す。

  ○ My American friend John is coming to Japan this fall.
  × An American friend of mine John is coming to Japan this fall.

❏ 場所の後の関係詞に使われる which

 場所の後の関係詞は必ず where と覚えてる学生がかなりいるが、先行詞が動詞の目的語になっている場合は which でないと誤りである。なお関係副詞の where は省けないが、この which は関係代名詞の目的格なので省略ができる。

  ○ This is the house where I was born.
  × This is the house which I was born.
  ○ This is the town (which) I like best.
  × This is the town where I like best.

用法上の注意

❏ 「立ち寄る」に相当する英語

 「立ち寄る」に相当する英語として drop in と stop over がよく使われるが、前者は「(ある場所に) ひょっこり立ち寄る、ちょっと立ち寄る」ときに使い、後者は「(旅行の途中などである場所に) 立ち寄る、途中で降りる」ときに用いられる。

  ○ Please drop in and see us when you come up to Tokyo.
  × Please stop over to see us when you come up to Tokyo.

- ○ The Chinese tourist stopped over in Tokyo on his way to New York.
- × The Chinese tourist dropped in Tokyo on his way to New York.

❑ 「旅」を意味する tour, trip, journey, travel の違い

tour は「数箇所を訪ねるような周遊旅行」、trip は「特定の目的である場所へ行って戻る旅」、journey は「特に陸路の比較的遠距離の旅」、travel は不加算名詞で「旅行一般」、常に複数形で用いられる travels は「国外旅行など、遠い所を訪れる長い旅」。

- ○ We're going on a ten-day tour of England this summer.
- × We're going on a ten-day travel of England this summer.
- ○ I made a business trip to China last week.
- ○ I don't like air travel.
- × I don't like air travels.
- ○ We saw a lot of wild animals on our travels in Africa.

❑ worth + ~ing

「～する価値がある」の英訳は「worth+ 動名詞」で「worth+ 不定詞」は誤り。

- ○ When you come to Japan, Kyoto is worth visiting.
- × When you come to Japan, Kyoto is worth to visit.

慣用表現を正しく覚えよう

be just around the corner 「すぐそこで、間近に迫って」
　Spring is just around the corner.

be brought up 「育てられる、育つ」
　He was born in China, but was brought up in Japan.

show someone around 「人に場所を案内して回る」
　Welcome to Kobe. I'll show you around the city tomorrow.

Exercise A

次の日本語 (A) に相当する英単語［句］を (B) より選び結びつけなさい。

(A)	(B)
1. 夏休み	1. college senior
2. 故郷の	2. on one's way home
3. 大学4年生	3. state
4. 観光旅行	4. be located
5. 帰途	5. native
6. 州	6. summer vacation
7. 位置する	7. sightseeing tour
8. 卒業論文	8. natural beauty
9. 国立公園	9. graduation thesis
10. 自然美	10. national park

Exercise B

次の文章の空所を埋めるのに適切な単語［句］をA, Bより選びなさい。

1. クリスマスはもうすぐで当地を訪れる観光客は増えています。

    Christmas is _____ and more and more tourists are visiting here.

    (A. just around the corner   B. soon around the corner)

2. 私の友人の1人が来月カナダへ行きます。

    _____ goes to Canada next month.

    (A. My friend   B. A friend of mine)

3. あなたの英語はとてもうまいのですね。アメリカで育ったのですか。

    Your English is very good. _____ in the United States?

    (A. Did you bring up   B. Were you brought up)

4. ロサンゼルスからの帰途ホノルルに立ち寄り、市内を観光しました。

    On my way home from Los Angeles, I (a) _____ Honolulu and (b) _____ of the city.

    (a) (A. dropped in   B. stopped over in)

    (b) (A. took a sightseeing tour   B. took a sightseeing travel)

5. 私が入りたい大学はスタンフォード大学です。

   The university _____ I would like to enter is Stanford.

   (A. where   B. which)

6. 横浜へ来たら私が案内して回りますよ。

   When you come to Yokohama, I'll _____ the city.

   (A. show you around   B. guide you)

7. 時間があればこの美術館は訪れる価値があります。

   This art museum is _____ if you have time.

   (A. worth to visit   B. worth visiting)

Exercise C

次の和文を英語に訳しなさい。

1. 旅行ほど楽しいものはありません。

2. 人々は豊かになるにつれ自分の国はもとより外国へも旅行に行きます。

3. 盛んな国際観光が、異なった文化や人々のよりよい理解に役立つのは確かです。

   「盛んな」flourishing

4. 日本政府は、最近、わが国への観光客を増やすために観光ビザの発給条件の緩和などさまざまな政策を講じています。

   「緩和する」ease ~ 「さまざまな政策を講じる」take various measures [steps]

5. 政府は、東京でオリンピックが開かれる2020年には、日本を訪れる人が4千万人を超えることを期待しています。

   「4千万人」40 million people

Flourishing International Tourism 5

UNIT 2
Increasing Popularity of Japanese Food Abroad

海外で高まる日本食の人気

日本食は、健康的なだけでなくおいしくて、見た目も美しいので、海外で人気が高まっている。外国人が、日本食へ関心を向け始めたのは1970年代中ごろで、最初はニューヨークやロサンゼルスなど日本人や日系人の多く住むアメリカの大都市で、芸能人や高所得者がお寿司をカロリーの低い健康食として食べ始めた。その後、日本食レストランが増えるにつれ、健康志向のオフィスワーカーたちも追随した。ロンドンやパリなどヨーロッパの大都市でも日本食を食べる人が増加した。今日では、お寿司のほかに、すきやき、てんぷら、焼き鳥なども好んで食べる外国人は多い。なお、和食、すなわち伝統的な日本食は、2013年12月に、ユネスコの無形文化遺産に選定された。

‖Warm-up‖

次の会話を聴いて空欄を埋めなさい。

Dialogue

A: I hear **an increasing number of** people in the United States and Europe as well as (   ) begin to take a great interest in Japanese **food**.

B: (   ). In the United States sushi first became **popular** among health-conscious people as a low-calorie food (   ). Today the varieties of Japanese **cuisine** Americans enjoy eating are increasing.

A: What are other Japanese dishes Americans like?

B: They range from sukiyaki to tempura, yakitori and ramen noodles.

A: (   ) Japanese food is so popular abroad?

B: **Because** Japanese food is not only well-balanced and **good for your health** but also beautiful. In addition, I feel (   ) makes the most of natural flavors.

A: No wonder "washoku," or traditional Japanese cuisine, is designated as an Intangible Cultural Heritage by UNESCO.

Notes:
health-conscious「健康志向の」／ **variety**「種類、品目」／ **cuisine**「料理」／ **dish**「食べ物、料理」／ **flavor**「味、風味」／ **traditional**「伝統的な」／ **designate**「選定する」／ **Intangible Cultural Heritage**「無形文化遺産」／ **no wonder**「不思議ではない、当然だ」／ **UNESCO** = United Nations Educational, Scientific and Cultural Organization「国際連合教育科学文化機関、ユネスコ」

文法上の注意

❏ an increasing number of ＋名詞に呼応するのは複数動詞

　　○ An increasing number of Japanese food restaurants have opened abroad since the beginning of this century.
　　× An increasing number of Japanese food restaurants has opened abroad since the beginning of this century.

❏ popular に続く前置詞

「(人に) 人気がある」を意味する popular に続く前置詞としては among も with も用いられる。among は、慣習、スポーツ、食べ物などが国民や大衆や多くの人々の間に広く浸透・流布している場合に好んでも使われる。一方 with は、対象が多くの人々のときもあるが、目的語は 1 人でもよい。

　　○ This food is very popular among young women.
　　○ This food is very popular with young women.
　　× This food is very popular to young women.
　　○ That actor is not very popular with me just now.

❏ because の正しい使い方

　　○ I didn't attend the meeting last night because I didn't feel well.
　　× I didn't attend the meeting last night. Because I didn't feel well.
　　○ "Why didn't you attend the meeting last night?" "Because I didn't feel well."

Because I didn't feel well. は従属節だけで完全な文章ではないので、このような表現が正用法となるのは Why で始まる疑問文に対する答えのときだけ。

用法上の注意

❏ food の使い方

food は「食べ物全般、または～料理」などを指すときは不可算名詞。特定の食べ物を指す場合のみ可算名詞。

- ○ I'm afraid we're running out of food.
- × I'm afraid we're running out of foods.
- ○ She bought a lot of packaged, easy-to-prepare foods the other day.
- × She bought a lot of packaged, easy-to-prepare food the other day.

❏ cuisine は常に不可算名詞

- ○ This hotel has a reputation for serving delicious Japanese cuisine.
- × This hotel has a reputation for serving delicious Japanese cuisines.

❏ 「健康に良い [悪い]」の英訳

「健康である [ない]」は be in good [bad] health だが、「健康に良い [悪い]」は be good [bad] for one's health で health の前には one's が必要。

- ○ Do you think jogging is good for our health?
- × Do you think jogging is good for health?
- ○ I hope your mother is in good health.
- × I hope your mother is in her good health.

慣用表現を正しく覚えよう

as well as ~「～だけでなく」
She likes Japanese food as well as French cuisine.

range from A to B「A から B までに及ぶ」
The participants in the festival ranged from children to elderly people.

in addition「さらに、そのうえ」
The Japanese food we are going to eat this evening is priced at ¥5,000. In addition, we have to pay the consumption tax.

make the most of ~「～を最大限活用する」
You should make the most of this golden opportunity.

Exercise A

次の日本語 (A) に相当する英単語 [句] を (B) より選び結びつけなさい。

(A)	(B)
1. 海外で	1. interest
2. 追加	2. health-conscious
3. 文化的な	3. intangible
4. 風味	4. heritage
5. 関心	5. abroad
6. 遺産	6. addition
7. 料理	7. flavor
8. 無形の	8. variety
9. 健康志向の	9. cultural
10. 品目	10. cuisine

Exercise B

次の文章の空所を埋めるのに適切な単語 [句] を A, B より選びなさい。

1. カリフォルニアには多くの日本食レストランがあります。

   _____ Japanese food restaurants in California.

   (A. There is a large number of   B. There are a large number of)

2. 今日ではアメリカ人ばかりでなく欧州の人々も日本料理にかなり関心を持っています。

   Today Europeans (a)_____ Americans take (b)_____ Japanese cuisine.

   (a) (A. as well as   B. as many as)

   (b) (A. a considerable interest in   B. considerable interest in)

3. これらの日本料理は私の料理のクラスの生徒たちに大変人気がある。

   These Japanese dishes are very _____ the students in my cooking class.   (A. popular to   B. popular with)

4. マイケルが良く食べる日本食はすきやきからラーメンにまで及んでいる。

   The variety of Japanese food Michael often eats _____ sukiyaki to ramen noodles.   (A. ranges   B. ranges from)

Increasing Popularity of Japanese Food Abroad

5. 日本食は健康に良いと考えられている。

   Japanese food is considered to be ＿＿＿＿＿＿＿＿.

   (A. healthy   B. good for our health)

6. 日本食はバランスが良く取れているばかりかおいしくて美しいので、多くの外国人に好まれるのは当然です。

   ＿＿＿＿＿＿＿＿ many foreigners like Japanese food; it's not only well-balanced but also delicious and beautiful.   (A. No wonder   B. No surprise)

7. 和食は2013年12月にユネスコにより無形文化遺産に選定された。

   In December 2013 "washoku" was designated by UNESCO as an ＿＿＿＿＿＿＿＿.

   (A. Intangible Cultural Heritage   B. Intangible Culture Heritage)

Exercise C

次の和文を英語に訳しなさい。

1. 日本食は、健康的なだけでなく、おいしくて見た目も美しいので、海外で人気が高まっています。

2. 外国人が、日本食へ関心を向け始めたのは1970年代の中頃です。

3. 最初は、ニューヨークやロサンゼルスなど日本人や日系アメリカ人の多く住むアメリカの大都市で、芸能人や高所得者が、お寿司をカロリーの低い健康食として食べ始めました。

   「芸能人や高所得者」entertainers and high-income earners

4. 日本食レストランが増えるにつれ、健康志向のオフィスワーカーも追随しました。

5. ユネスコは、2013年12月に、「和食」、すなわち伝統的な日本食を無形文化遺産に選定しました。

UNIT 3
Homestay

ホームステイ

ホームステイは、学生や旅行者が外国の家庭に滞在してその国の言葉や生活様式や習慣などを学ぶ制度で、近年この制度を利用して海外へ行く日本人や日本に来る外国人が増加している。ホームステイする人は、お客としてではなくホストファミリーの一員とみなされるので異文化にじかに触れることができる。ホームステイを経験した人は、異文化間コミュニケーションの機会がますます増えるこれからの世界で、重要な役割を担うようになるだろう。

Warm-up

次の会話を聴いて空欄を埋めなさい。

Dialogue

A: **Have you ever stayed** in (   )?

B: Yes, I have. When I was a freshman at college, I participated in a **homestay** program and (   ) in the United States.

A: How was your homestay? Did you **have any difficulty** speak**ing** and understanding English?

B: Well, I didn't have much difficulty making myself understood in English, but **at first** I had some trouble understanding what the college student in my homestay family said because he used lots of **slang**.

A: I see. Did you get used to an American way of life (   )?

B: Before I did a homestay, I had been told that I would be treated not as a guest but (   ) the homestay family, but since I didn't do any household chores when I was in Japan, I was quite embarrassed when I had to do the dishes with the children in my host family.

A: I stayed with a Japanese family for a month, and found that a homestay is a very effective way of learning **the Japanese language** and catching a glimpse of everyday family life.

B: Living with a family in a foreign country is certainly one of the best ways to (　　　　　　　　　　　　).

Notes:
freshman「1年生」/ **way of life**「生活様式」/ **treat**「待遇する」/ **household chores**「家事」/ **be embarrassed**「困惑する」/ **do the dishes**「皿洗いする」/ **effective**「効果的な」/ **catch a glimpse of ~**「～を垣間見る」

文法上の注意

❏ 経験を表す現在完了

英語では現在までの経験を表すのには、その経験が起こったのが過去のいつであれ、現在完了時制が用いられる

- ○ Have you ever made an overseas trip?
- × Did you ever make an overseas trip?
- ○ We have lived in this house since 2001.
- × We live in this house since 2001.

❏ have difficulty [trouble] + ~ing

「～するのに苦労する」は昔は have difficulty [trouble] in + ~ing の型を取っていたが、近年では in を省いて使われることが多い。特に略式体や会話ではこの傾向が強い。

- ○ Do you have any difficulty [trouble] in speaking Japanese?
- ○ Do you have any difficulty [trouble] speaking Japanese?

用法上の注意

❏ homestay

homestay という語は英和辞典によっては不加算名詞としているものもある（e.g. ロングマン英和辞典）が、可算名詞としても用いられる。また自動詞の用例を載せている辞書もある（e.g. スーパー・アンカー英和辞典）が、「ホームステイする」は do a homestay が一般的で、homestay はあまり自動詞としては用いられていないようである。homestay という語は、英語圏で使われる場合は、homestay program とか homestay experience など形容詞的な用法が多い。

❏ at first と first の違い

at first と first を間違って使う人が多いが、at first は「最初は」、first は順番を述べるときの「最初に」である。

- ○ First, mix the egg and milk, and then add the flour.
- × At first, mix the egg and milk, and then add the flour.
- ○ At first, I didn't like the climate in Japan, but as I stayed longer, I got used to it.
- × First, I didn't like the climate in Japan, but as I stayed longer, I got used to it.

❏ 「スラング」は不加算名詞

- ○ Peter uses a lot of slang.
- × Peter uses a lot of slangs.

❏ 「日本語」は Japanese か the Japanese language

「〜語」に language を使う場合は必ず定冠詞が付く。

- ○ He is good at Japanese.
- ○ He is good at the Japanese language.
- × He is good at the Japanese.
- × He is good at Japanese language.

慣用表現を正しく覚えよう

make oneself understood「自分の言いたいことを分かってもらう」

Can you make yourself understood in English?

get used to ~「〜に慣れる」

get used to の後には名詞か動名詞で、「〜することに慣れる」の英訳で to- 不定詞を使うのは誤り。

It took Mary quite some time to get used to her new life in England.

Have you gotten used to making a speech in public?

Exercise A

次の日本語 (A) に相当する英単語 [句] を (B) より選び結びつけなさい。

1. 一見
2. 困惑する
3. 向上する
4. 待遇する
5. 文化
6. 家事
7. 生活様式
8. 困難
9. 効果的な
10. 一年生

1. culture
2. difficulty
3. freshman
4. way of life
5. improve
6. treat
7. household chores
8. be embarrassed
9. effective
10. glimpse

Exercise B

次の文章の空所を埋めるのに適切な単語 [句] をA, B より選びなさい。

1. 私は西北大学の1年生です。
   I'm a _____ at Seihoku University.　(A. first student　B. freshman)

2. これまでにホームステイプログラムに参加したことはありますか。
   _____ in a homestay program?
   (A. Have you ever participated　B. Did you ever participate)

3. カナダのホストファミリーと生活して英語を話すのに慣れましたか。
   As a result of staying with a Canadian host family, _____?
   (A. have you gotten used to speak English　B. have you gotten used to speaking English)

4. アメリカの学生たちはスラングをたくさん使います。
   American students use lots of _____.　(A. slang　B. slangs)

5. 初めてオーストラリアでホームステイしたとき、夕食後皿洗いするのに困惑しました。
   When I (a)_____ stayed with an Australian family, I (b)_____ to do the dishes after dinner.
   　(a) (A. at first　B. first)　(b) (A. embarrassed　B. was embarrassed)

6. ホームステイの経験は英語を向上させるのにまたとない機会を与えてくれるでしょう。

   A homestay experience will _____ a unique opportunity to improve your English.

   (A. provide you   B. provide you with)

7. ホームステイは異文化を学ぶ最もよい方法の1つです。

   A homestay is _____ of learning different cultures.

   (A. one of the best way   B. one of the best ways)

Exercise C

次の和文を英語に訳しなさい。

1. ホームステイは、学生や旅行者が外国の家庭に滞在し、その国の言葉や習慣や生活様式などを学ぶプログラムです。

2. 近年ホームステイプログラムに参加する日本人や外国人が増えています。

3. ホームステイする人はお客ではなく家族の1員とみなされます。

4. ホームステイプログラムは、参加者に、異文化にじかに接するまたとない機会を提供します。
   「またとない機会」a unique opportunity

5. 異文化間コミュニケーションの機会がますます増えるのは確実で、ホームステイを経験した人々はこれからの世界で重要な役割を担うようになるでしょう。
   「異文化間コミュニケーション」cross-cultural communications

UNIT 4
The Olympic Games and the Paralympic Games

オリンピックとパラリンピック大会

第1回のオリンピック大会は1896年にギリシャのアテネで開催された。一方、公式のパラリンピック大会は1960年にイタリヤのローマで、23か国から400人の選手が参加して行われました。1989年に非営利団体として設立された国際パラリンピック委員会はパラリンピック運動の世界的な統治機関です。1988年のソウル大会以降パラリンピック大会は4年ごとにオリンピック大会と同じ年に同じ場所で行われ、大会に参加する選手と国は急速に増えてきています。

⫼Warm-up⫼

次の会話を聴いて空欄を埋めなさい。

Dialogue

A: We (　　　　　　) about the Olympic Games, but we don't know **much** about the Paralympic Games, do we?

B: (　　　　　　). What are the Paralympic Games?

A: Well, they're (　　　　　　　　　) in which **a number of athletes** with a range of physical disabilities **participate**.

B: When are they held?

A: They're held (　　　　　　)—in the same year as the Olympic Games.

B: (　　　　　　) the next Paralympic Games will **be held** in Tokyo in

2020 since the Japanese capital was selected as the host city at the IOC's 125th session. The IOC stands for the International Olympic Committee.

A: I'm looking forward to seeing both the Olympics and the Paralympics in Tokyo.

Notes:
a range of「いろいろな」／ **athlete**「運動選手」／ **physical disability**「身体障害」／ **capital**「首都」／ **select**「選出する」／ **host city**「開催都市」／ **session**「大会」／ **the International Olympic Committee**「国際オリンピック委員会」

文法上の注意

❏ much の正しい使い方

much は主として疑問文と否定文で用いられ、as, so, too や very の後などを除いて通例肯定文では使えない。

○ I don't like him because he talks too much.
○ I don't like him because he talks a lot.
× I don't like him because he talks much.

❏ a number of + 複数名詞 + 複数動詞と the number of + 複数名詞 + 単数動詞

a number of + 複数名詞 は複数動詞で、the number of + 複数名詞は単数動詞で呼応。

○ A number of students plan to participate in the anti-war demonstration.
× A number of students plans to participate in the anti-war demonstration.
○ On the weekends the number of travelers is very large.
× On the weekend the number of travelers are very large.

用法上の注意

❏ athlete と player

athlete も player も「運動選手」を意味するが、player は野球やサッカーなどの球技をする選手に限定して用いられる。水泳の選手は swimmer。

○ How many athletes are going to participate in the coming Paralympics?
× How many players are going to participate in the coming Paralympics?
○ How many players are going to participate in the coming table tennis tournament?

❏ participate in ~ と join

日本語の「〜に参加する」に相当する英語には take part [participate] in ~ と join があるが、両者は区別され、競技会やトーナメントなどに参加する場合は前者、団体など参加するは後者が用いられる。

- ○ He took part [participated] in the U.S. Open Tennis Championships last year.
- × He joined the U.S. Open Tennis Championships last year.
- ○ She joined the women's chorus because she liked singing.
- × She took part [participated] in the women's chorus because she liked singing.

❏ hold と open

「開く」に相当する英単語には hold と open があるが、「開催する」の意味のときは hold で、open は「始める」の意で用いられる。

- ○ The next meeting will be held in a week.
- × The next meeting will be opened in a week.
- ○ We would like to open tonight's meeting with a word from our president.
- × We would like to hold tonight's meeting with a word from our president.

慣用表現を正しく覚えよう

take part in ~ = participate in ~「〜に参加する」
How many countries are expected to take part in the Tokyo Olympics?

look forward to ~ing [動名詞]「〜するのを楽しみにしている」
この to は不定詞を導く to ではなく次には名詞または動名詞が続く。
We are all looking forward to meeting the many foreign visitors who will come to see the Tokyo Olympics and Paralympics.

stand for ~「〜の略です」
What does ATM stand for? It stands for the automated teller machine.

Exercise A

次の日本語 (A) に相当する英単語［句］を (B) より選び結びつけなさい。

(A)	(B)
1. 国際競技大会	1. capital
2. 身体障害	2. participant
3. 非営利団体	3. nonprofit organization
4. 国際パラリンピック委員会	4. select
5. パラリンピック運動	5. competition
6. 参加者	6. physical disability
7. 首都	7. international event
8. 選出する	8. Paralympic Movement
9. 大会	9. session
10. 競争	10. International Paralympic Committee

Exercise B

次の文章の空所を埋めるのに適切な単語［句］を A, B より選びなさい。

1. 次回のパラリンピク大会に参加する選手は5千人を超えると思われます。
   (a)＿＿＿＿＿＿ of athletes to participate in the coming Paralympics
   (b)＿＿＿＿＿＿ expected to surpass 5,000.
   (a) (A. A number　B. The number)　(b) (A. are　B. is)

2. 彼は北京のオリンピックの男子シングルスで優勝したテニスの選手です。
   He is the tennis ＿＿＿＿＿＿ who won the men's singles championship in the Olympic Games in Beijing.　(A. athlete　B. player)

3. 何人の選手が女子100メートルバタフライにエントリーしてますか。
   How many ＿＿＿＿＿＿ have entered the women's 100-meter butterfly race?　(A. players　B. swimmers)

4. 冬季オリンピック大会は雪の多い地方で開催されます。
   The Winter Olympic Games ＿＿＿＿＿＿ in an area which has lots of snow.
   (A. are opened　B. are held)

The Olympic Games and the Paralympic Games　19

5. 日本が最初にオリンピックに参加したのはいつですか。

When did Japan first _____ the Olympic Games?
　（A. join　B. participate in）

6. JOC は何の略ですか。

What does JOC _____?　（A. stand for　B. stand by）

7. 彼は今度のパラリンピックでアメリカのライバルと戦うのを期待して待っています。

He is _____ with his American rival in the coming Paralympics.
　（A. looking forward to compete　B. looking forward to competing）

Exercise C

次の和文を英語に訳しなさい。

1. 第1回の近代オリンピック大会は、1896年に、ギリシャのアテネで開催されました。

2. パラリンピック大会は、1948年にイギリスで行われたスポーツ大会が起源だと言われています。

3. 初めての公式のパラリンピック大会は、1960年にローマで、23カ国から400人の選手が参加し行われました。

4. 1989年に非営利益団体として設立された国際パラリンピック委員会はパラリンピック大会の世界的な統治機関です。

　「統治機関」governing body

5. 今日、パラリンピック大会は、4年ごとに、オリンピック大会と同じ年に同じ場所で行われます。

UNIT 5
The Nobel Prize

ノーベル賞

ノーベル賞は、ダイナマイトの発明者として知られるスウェーデン人アルフレッド・ノーベルの遺言に従って1895年に創設され、1901年から授与が始まった。最初は、物理学、化学、生理・医学、文学、平和の5分野で顕著な功績を残した人に贈られてきたが、1968年にノーベル経済学賞が設立され、現在6分野で授賞が行われている。1949年に、物理学者の湯川秀樹博士が日本人としては初めてノーベル賞を受賞して以来2016年までに、25人の日本人(日本で生まれ国籍を米国に移した人を含む)がこの栄誉に浴している。内訳は11人が物理学、7人が化学、3人が生理・医学、2人が文学、1人が平和の分野でノーベル賞を受賞している。21世紀以降、自然科学の分野ではノーベル賞受賞の数は日本はアメリカに次いで2位である。

‖Warm-up‖

次の会話を聴いて空欄を埋めなさい。

Dialogue

A: It's amazing that Japan has produced Nobel Prize winners for three years in a row.

B: (　　　　　　　　) that Dr. Satoshi Omura won the Nobel Prize in 2015 in Physiology or Medicine for developing medicines (　　　　　　　　) to treat parasitic **diseases**, particularly in Africa and South Asia. He has saved more than 200 million people from becoming blind. I read a couple of books about him and was deeply impressed by his way of thinking.

A: What's his way of thinking?

B: He grew up on a farm and (　　　　　　　　　　　　　) in his childhood. He believes nature has all the answers to our problems and **that** micro-organisms are limitless resources capable of meeting our requirements. He always tells his students (   ) making mistakes because it's his belief that success usually comes after a series of failures.

A: I read in the paper the other day that his mother had always told him (   ) for society.

B: He has faithfully followed his mother's advice and made brilliant achievements in medicine.

Notes:
amazing「驚くべき」/ **produce**「輩出する」/ **winner**「受賞者」/ **Nobel Prize in Physiology or Medicine**「ノーベル生理・医学賞」/ **medicine**「薬」/ **treat**「治療する」/ **parasitic disease**「寄生虫病」/ **blind**「盲目の、目の見えない」/ **a couple of**「2、3の」/ **be impressed**「感銘を受ける」/ **farm**「農場」/ **childhood**「子供時代、幼年時代」/ **microorganism**「微生物」/ **limitless**「無限の、限りない」/ **resource**「資源」/ **capable of ~ing**「~することができる」/ **requirement**「要件、要求」/ **success**「成功」/ **failure**「失敗」/ **paper** = newspaper「新聞」/ **faithfully**「忠実に」/ **brilliant**「輝かしい」/ **achievement**「業績」

文法上の注意

❏ 接続詞 that の正しい使い方

believe, say, think などの動詞が目的節を導くときは that を省略することがよくあるが、2つの等位文節では、第1節の前に that がなくてもに、第2節の前では文意を明確にするために that を入れないといけない。

「彼は母は休暇でカナダへ行っているけど、父はスケジュールが忙しく東京にいると言っています」

○ He says his mother has gone to Canada on vacation, but that his father is in Tokyo because of his busy schedule.

× He says his mother has gone to Canada on vacation, but his father is in Tokyo because of his busy schedule.

2番目の文章だと「父は東京にいる」のは彼が言っているのか、それとも彼の発言とは関係なく彼の父が東京にいるのか不明確である。

用法上の注意

❏ disease と illness

日本語の「病気」に相当する英語には disease と illness があるが、前者は病名が付いていたり、ウイルスや細菌が原因で伝染する病気、後者は病気であるときの一般的な状態を示す。

- ○ Is AIDS a contagious disease?
- × Is AIDS a contagious illness?
- ○ Illness prevented me from attending the meeting last night.
- × Disease prevented me from attending the meeting last night.

❏ advice は不可算名詞

日本語だと「忠告」は加算名詞のように思えるが、英語の advice は不加算名詞。どうしても数えたいときには piece を使う。

- ○ You should take your brother's advice.
- × You should take your brother's advices.
- ○ I'll give you two pieces of good advice.
- × I'll give you two good advice.

慣用表現を正しく覚えよう

in a row「連続して、続けて」
  We have unusual weather. It's been raining five days in a row.

way of thinking「考え方」
  I think his way of thinking is out of date.

grow up「育つ、成長する、大人になる」
  What would you like to be when you grow up?

the other day「先日」
  An American friend of mine took me to lunch the other day.

Exercise A

次の日本語 (A) に相当する英単語 [句] を (B) より選び結びつけなさい。

(A)	(B)
1. 病気	1. achievement
2. 開発する	2. success
3. 治療する	3. failure
4. 子供時代	4. disease
5. 業績	5. medicine
6. 資源	6. treat
7. 成功	7. develop
8. 失敗	8. childhood
9. 化学	9. resource
10. 医学	10. chemistry

Exercise B

次の文章の空所を埋めるのに適切な単語 [句] を A, B より選びなさい。

1. 日本は3年連続でノーベル賞受賞者を出しました。

   Japan has produced Nobel Prize winners for three years _____.
   　(A. in a row　B. in row)

2. 大村博士は寄生虫病治療薬の開発でノーベル生理・医学賞を授与されました。

   Dr. Omura was awarded the Nobel Prize in Physiology or Medicine for developing
   　(a) _____ to treat parasitic (b)_____.
   　(a) (A. medicine　B. medicines)　(b) (A. illnesses　B. diseases)

3. 大村博士は2億人以上の人々を盲目から救った。

   Dr. Omura saved more than 200 million people _____ blind.
   　(A. from becoming　B. to become)

4. 大村博士に関する本を数冊読んで私は彼の考え方に大変感激しました。

   I read a couple of books (a)_____ him and was deeply impressed by his (b) _____.
   　(a) (A. about　B. by)　(b) (A. way of thinking　B. way to think)

5. 彼は農場で育ち、幼年時代から自然に親しんできた。

   He (a) _____ on a farm and lived (b)_____ in his (c)_____.

   (a) (A. was grown up B. grew up)   (b) (A. close to nature   B. kind to nature)
   (c) (A. child   B. childhood)

6. 彼は微生物はわれわれの要求を満たすことのできる無限の資源であると信じています。

   He believes that microorganisms are limitless resources _____ our needs.　　　　　　　　　　　　　　(A. capable of meeting   B. able to meet)

7. 彼は母親の忠告を忠実に守り医学の分野で輝かしい業績を上げました。

   Faithfully (a) _____ his mother's (b)_____, he has made brilliant achievements in the field of medicine.

   (a) (A. protecting   B. following)   (b) (A. advice   B. advices)

Exercise C

次の和文を英語に訳しなさい。

1. ノーベル賞は、ダイナマイトの発明者であるスウェーデン人アルフレッド・ノーベルの遺言に従って1895年に創設されました。　　　「ダイナマイト」dynamite 「遺言」will

2. 最初は、ノーベル賞は物理学、化学、生理学、医学、文学、平和の5分野で顕著な功績を上げた人々に贈られていました。今日では経済科学を含む6分野で授賞が行われています。

3. 1949年に、物理学者の湯川秀樹は博士が、日本人としては初めてノーベル賞を受賞しました。

4. 2016年末時点で、25人の日本人（日本で生まれたが国籍をアメリカに移した人を含む）がノーベル賞受賞の栄誉に浴しています。

5. 21世紀では、自然科学の分野のノーベル賞受賞者は、日本はアメリカについで2位です。

UNIT 6
Keeping in Shape

健康維持

太りすぎが健康に悪いことはよく知られている。肥満は糖尿病や心臓病やある種のガンを誘発することがあると言う。しかし都会に住む人は運動不足から体重過多になることがよくある。体重を減らすためにダイエットする人はかなりいるようだがあまり成功した例は聞かない。体重を減らし健康を保つにはジムに通って運動するのもよいが、これはかなりお金がかかる。最も簡単で最も安価な健康維持の方法は歩くことで、最近散歩に精を出している人をよく見かける。

‖Warm-up‖

次の会話を聴いて空欄を埋めなさい。

Dialogue

A: Hi, Kimiko. How are things going?

B: Hi, Ben. Things **could** be (   ).

A: What's the matter? Do you have problems at school?

B: No. The trouble is my weight. I've gained five kilos (   ) and I'm not in good shape.

A: I know too much weight is bad for your health. Have you made any efforts to lose weight?

B: First I went on a diet for two months and lost seven kilos, but as soon as I gave up the diet, I (   ). Then I became a member of a fitness club and did **exercise** three times a week, but when I got **busy studying**, the club membership was unused for several weeks. It was just a waste of money, and I quit.

A: I **suggest you take** a walk for an hour or so every day. You see lots of people walking near our campus every morning and evening, don't you? Most of them look very healthy. Since your apartment is only two kilometers from our campus, you should (   ). Walking is the best and cheapest way to keep in shape. It allows people to (   ) in a short period of time.

Notes:
How are things going?「調子はどう？、うまくやっいる？」/ **What's the matter?**「どうしたの？」/ **problem**「問題」/ **trouble**「問題」/ **gain**「増える」/ **effort**「努力」/ **membership**「会員資格」/ **waste**「浪費」/ **quit**「辞める」/ **healthy**「健康そうな」/ **allow**「〜を可能にする」

文法上の注意

❏ could は可能性を表すことがある

could は能力だけでなく、可能性を表す場合にも用いられるので、Things could be a lot better. は「調子はもっとずっとよくてもよいのだが、実際はよくない」という意味になる。

❏ busy + ~ing

「〜するのに忙しい」は、かつては「busy in + ~ing」の型を取っていたが、今日では「busy + ~ing」のほうが一般的である。なお、「busy + to 不定詞」は誤り。
　○ I'm busy doing my homework now.
　× I'm busy to do my homework now.

❏ suggest の使い方

米用法では suggest が that 節を伴って使われるときは that 節の中の動詞は仮定法現在。
　○ His professor suggested that he write about his experiences in China.
　○ His professor suggested that he should write about his experiences in China.
　　（主として英用法）
　× His professor suggested that he writes about his experiences in China.

用法上の注意

❏ exercise と exercises

単に「運動する」と言う場合は do [get, take] exercise で、exercise は不加算名詞。ただし「呼吸運動」とか「屈伸運動」のように個別の運動を指すときは可算名詞として用いられる。

- ○ I do exercise every morning to keep in shape.
- × I do exercises every morning to keep in shape.
- ○ I do stretching exercises before I go to bed.
- × I do stretching exercise before I go to bed.

慣用表現を正しく覚えよう

be in good shape「体調が良い、健康である」
　My parents are in good shape.
be on a diet「ダイエットをしている、ダイエット中」
　My sister is on a diet to lose weight.
　「ダイエットをする」は go on a diet
give up「(薬・飲み物・ダイエットなどを) 止める」
　He gave up smoking because it was bad for his health.
keep in shape「体調 [健康] を保つ」
　She goes for a two-kilometer jog every morning to keep in shape.
　「体調 [健康] を保つ」は stay in shape とも言う。

Exercise A

次の日本語 (A) に相当する英単語 [句] を (B) より選び結びつけなさい。

(A)	(B)
1. 体重	1. way
2. 健康	2. near
3. 問題	3. be in good shape
4. 体調が良い	4. health
5. 浪費	5. membership
6. 方法	6. gain
7. 会員資格	7. problem
8. 運動	8. weight
9. 増える	9. exercise
10. 近く	10. waste

Exercise B

次の文章の空所を埋めるのに適切な単語 [句] を A, B より選びなさい。

1. 私は仕事で忙しい。

   I am busy _____.

   (A. to work   B. working)

2. 調子はあまりよくないよ。

   Things _____ a lot better.

   (A. could be   B. should be)

3. 太りすぎは体に良くない。

   Too much weight is not good _____.

   (A. for health   B. for your health)

4. 私は今年の初めに1ヶ月ダイエットをしていました。

   I _____ for a month at the beginning of this year.

   (A. was on a diet   B. was on diet)

5. ダイエットを止めたとき、体重は元に戻ってしまいました。

   When I (a)＿＿＿＿＿＿＿＿ the diet, I (b)＿＿＿＿＿＿＿＿.

   (a) (A. gave up   B. came out)

   (b) (A. put all the weight back   B. put all the weight back on)

6. 最近私はフィットネスクラブのメンバーになり週5回運動しています。

   I have recently become a member of a fitness club and ＿＿＿＿＿＿＿＿ five times a week.

   (A. do exercise   B. do exercises)

7. 私は健康を保つために毎日歩いています。

   I walk every day to ＿＿＿＿＿＿＿＿.

   (A. keep in health   B. keep in shape)

Exercise C

次の和文を英語に訳しなさい。

1. 体重過多が体に悪いことはよく知られています。

2. 肥満は糖尿病や心臓病やある種のガンを誘発することがあります。

   「肥満」obesity　「糖尿病」diabetes　「心臓病」heart disease　「ガン」cancer　「～を誘発する」lead to ～

3. 体重を減らすためにダイエットをする人はかなりいます。

4. フィットネスクラブで運動するのも健康を保つ方法の1つですが、これにはかなりお金がかかります。

5. 私は、お年寄りの方々が健康のために近所の公園を散歩しているのをよく見かけます。

UNIT 7
Job Hunting

就職活動

アメリカや多くの欧州諸国と違って、日本では通例学年度は4月1日に始まり3月31日に終わる。ほとんどの日本の企業は大学生が卒業する1年以上前から新規採用のプログラムを一斉に行うので、多くの大学生は3年生のうちから就職活動を始め、大学最終年の勉強をおろそかにしがちだ。

政府は「大学生は学業を優先すべきである」との方針から、大手の企業が加入する経団連に採用選考開始を遅らせ大学生の就職活動期間をなるべく短くするよう求めてきたが、経団連や大学との意見の相違は大きく、この開始日が最近すでに2回も変更になっているにもかかわらず、問題は根本的には解決していない。

日本ではまだ大企業や公務員希望の学生が多いが、大きな組織の中のほんの小さな歯車の1つになってしまい、自分の能力を十分に発揮できないこともよくある。就職先を決めるのにはいくら慎重になっても慎重すぎることはない。

‖Warm-up‖

次の会話を聴いて空欄を埋めなさい。

Dialogue

A: Have you started job hunting?

B: No, (　　　　　). I can't decide whether I should go on to graduate school or get a job after **graduating from** college. I'll probably make a final decision after I come back from **a three-week trip** to Europe.

A: A lucky guy! I've been struggling to find a job these few weeks, but I (　　　　　　　　　　　　　). I passed the written exams of the two large publishing companies **to** which I had **applied**, but I was **so** uptight at my job interviews, I couldn't sell myself.

B: (   ) are you looking for?

A: I've been studying English very hard in college, so (   ) where I can put my English knowledge to good use.

B: **Why not** apply to the newspaper company where my uncle is the personnel manager? I know (   ). I'll put in a good word for you. I'm sure he'll duly assess your competence.

A: Thank you. I really appreciate your kindness.

Notes:
job hunting「職探し、就職活動」／ **graduate school**「大学院」／ **probably**「多分」／ **final**「最終的な」／ **struggle to do**「～しようと努力する」／ **publishing company**「出版社」／ **uptight**「緊張した」／ **job interview**「就職面接」／ **personnel manager**「人事部長」／ **duly**「正当に」／ **assess**「評価する」／ **competence**「能力、適正」／ **appreciate**「感謝する」

文法上の注意

❏ a three-week trip

複数の数字が次に来る名詞とハイフンで繋がれ形容詞として用いられるときは名詞は単数形でないといけない。

- ○ He takes a two-hour piano lesson every week.
- × He takes a two-hours piano lesson every week.

❏ so...that.... 構文における that の省略

相関接続詞の so ... that ... 構文では、形式張らない文や口語では that がよく省略される。

- ○ I was so busy looking for a job that I didn't have much time to study for the past few weeks.
- ○ I was so busy looking for a job, I didn't have much time to study for the past few weeks. (informal or colloquial)

用法上の注意

❏ graduate の使い方

graduate が「卒業する」を意味するときは自動詞で、「大学を卒業する」は標準用法では graduate from college で、graduate college や be graduated from college は誤りとされている。

- ○ When did you graduate from college?
- × When did you graduate college?
- × When were you graduated from college?

❏ apply の使い方

「出願する」を意味する apply は対象が大学や会社のときはその後の前置詞は to で、対象が過程や仕事のときは前置詞は for。

- ○ She has applied to Kyoto University.
- × She has applied for Kyoto University.
- ○ I'll apply for the job you have recommended.
- × I'll apply to the job you have recommended.

なお、会社に仕事を申請するとき apply for a job with a company も使われる。

- ○ I'm going to apply for a job with my uncle's company.

❏ Why not...? は人に何かを勧める表現

Why not...? は提案・勧誘のみに用いられ、理由を尋ねる疑問文では使わない。

- ○ （人事部長に電話をしたらどうですか）　Why not call the personnel manager?
- × （なぜ人事部長に電話をしないのですか）　Why not call the personnel manager?
- ○ （なぜ人事部長に電話をしないのですか）
    Why do you not call the personnel manager?

慣用表現を正しく覚えよう

sell oneself「自分を売り込む、自己宣伝する」
　You need to sell yourself to get a promotion.
put ~ to good use「～を有効に使う、～を生かす」
　You should put your engineering skills to good use.
put in a good word for ~「～のために口添えする、～のことを推薦する」
　If you could put in a good word for me, I think I might get that job.

Exercise A

次の日本語 (A) に相当する英単語 [句] を (B) より選び結びつけなさい。

	(A)		(B)
1.	出版社	1.	knowledge
2.	就職面接	2.	apply
3.	知識	3.	appreciate
4.	人事部長	4.	assess
5.	適正	5.	publishing company
6.	応募する	6.	uptight
7.	評価する	7.	personnel manager
8.	感謝する	8.	duly
9.	正当に	9.	job interview
10.	緊張した	10.	competence

Exercise B

次の文章の空所を埋めるのに適切な単語 [句] を A, B より選びなさい。

1. 大学を卒業したら出版社で働きます。
   I'll (a) _____ a publishing company after I (b) _____ college.
   　(a) (A. work at　B. work for)　(b) (A. graduate　B. graduate from)

2. 彼はニューヨークヤンキースと 5 年契約を結んだ。
   He has concluded a _____ with the New York Yankees.
   　(A. five-year contract　B. five-years contract)

3. 私は日本の大手商社の 1 つに就職を申し込みました。
   I have applied (a) _____ a job (b) _____ one of Japan's leading trading companies.　(a) (A. for　B. to)　(b) (A. for　B. with)

4. どんな仕事をお探しですか。
   　What kind of job are you _____.　(A. looking　B. looking for)

5. 私は自分のマーケティング技術が生かせる仕事につきたい。

   I'd like to get a job where I can (a) _____ my marketing skills (b) _____.　(a) (A. make　B. put)　(b) (A. good use　B. to good use)

6. あなたは英語に精通しているから、英字新聞社に出願したらどう。

   Since you have (a) _____ English, (b) _____ apply to an English newspaper company?　(a) (A. a good knowledge in　B. a good knowledge of)　(b) (A. why not　B. why do you)

7. もし君がその仕事に尽きたいなら上司に君のことを推薦してあげるよ。

   If you want to get that job, I'll _____ you with my boss.
   　(A. put in a good word for　B. drop in a good word for)

Exercise C

次の和文を英語に訳しなさい。

1. 日本では、大多数の企業が、大学生が卒業する1年前から新規採用のプログラムを一斉に行います。　「一斉に」all at one time

2. 多くの大学生は、3年のうちから就職活動を始め、大学最終年の勉強をおろそかにしがちです。

3. 政府は、大学生は学業を最優先すべきであるとの信念から、経団連に採用選考開始を遅らせ大学生の就職活動期間をなるべく短くするよう求めてきました。
   　「経団連」the Federation of Economic Organizations　「～に求める」call on ~
   　「採用選考」employment screening

4. 日本ではまだ大企業や公務員希望の学生が多いが、大きな組織の中のほんの小さな歯車になってしまい、自分の能力を十分に発揮できないこともよくあります。
   　「公務員」civil servant　「組織の中の歯車」a cog in the machine [wheel]　「能力を発揮する」take one's talents to good advantage

5. 就職先を決めるのにはいくら慎重になっても慎重すぎることはありません。

UNIT 8
University Reform

大学改革

日本の大学の国際評価は低い。権威のあるイギリスの教育専門誌である The Times Higher Education が発表した 2015–2016 年の世界大学ランキングでは東京大学は 43 位で、京都大学は 88 位である。国際競争力が激化する中で、大学改革を断行して、国際的に活躍する人材を育成することは今日日本が直面している緊急の課題の 1 つである。その一環として、近年いくつかの大学で、すべての学生に、海外実習を義務づけたり、外国人教師を増やして専門科目の授業を英語で行い、優秀な学生を世界中海外からも引き付けて、次世代の世界のリーダーを育てようとする試みなどが始まっている。

Warm-up

次の会話を聴いて空欄を埋めなさい。

Dialogue

A: **What** do you think of Japanese education?

B: From my experience of attending high school in Aomori Prefecture for a year, I can say Japanese education is "passive learning."

A: What do you mean by "passive learning?"

B: (   ), students just **listen to** and (   ) and have **few** chances to express their opinions. I think (   ) are very important in education.

A: Well, one **reason** why discussions don't play an important part in Japanese education **is that** admission to most of (   ) is heavily based on (   ). In fact, when I entered this university, I didn't have any oral exams.

B: Then, Japanese universities should change their **admissions policies** so that education is more active and creative.

Notes:
university reform「大学改革」／ **experience**「経験」／ **passive**「受身の」／ **express**「表現する、述べる」／ **opinion**「意見」／ **oral exam**「口答試験、面接試験」exam は examination の略。**active**「積極的な、能動的な」／ **creative**「創造的な」

文法上の注意

❑ reason ... is because ... は正用法か

標準文法では「…の理由は…である」は reason ... is that ... ただし略式文や話し言葉では reason ... is because ... もよく使われている。

- ○ The only reason for taking the advanced English course is that I would like to study in American graduate school. (formal)
- ○ The only reason for taking the advanced English course is because I would like to study in American graduate school. (informal or colloquial)

用法上の注意

❑ 日本語の「どう」は英語ではいつも "how" か

日本語の「どう」は英語では多くの場合 "how" だが、いつも "how" とは限らない。

    どうやって教育制度をいろいろ改革するのですか。
- ○ How do you carry out various reforms in the educational system?

    あなたの苗字はどういうスペルですか。
- ○ How do you spell your family name?

    A と B はどう違うのですか。
- ○ What is the difference between A and B?
- × How is the difference between A and B?

    それはどういう意味ですか。
- ○ What do you mean by that?
- × How do you mean by that?

❏ listen to と hear はどう違う

一般的には、hear が「(音を) 耳で感知する、(音が) 聞こえてくる」であるのに対し listen to は「自分の方から耳を傾ける」の意。

○ Listen to what the teacher says.
× Hear what the teacher says.

❏ a few と few の違い

a few も few も数に言及して用いられるが、a few は「少しある [いる]」と肯定的、few は「ほとんどない [いない]」と否定的な意味で用いられる。

○ It will take a few minutes to walk to school.
× It will take few minutes to walk to school.
○ His lecture is so difficult that few students would understand it.
○ His lecture is so difficult that only a few students would understand it.
× His lecture is so difficult that a few students would understand it.

❏ admission と admissions の違い

「入学、入学許可」は admission と不可算名詞。「入学に関すること、入学者数」は admissions と複数形。

○ Goro and I are applying for admission to Stanford.
× Goro and I are applying for admissions to Stanford.
○ Our university has a very selective admissions policy.
× Our university has a very selective admission policy.

慣用表現を正しく覚えよう

What do you mean by ~?「～はどういう意味ですか、～とはどういうことですか」
　What do you mean by a "third party?"

write down「書き留める」
　Please write down your impressions of Canada.

play a part「役割を果たす」
　Wood plays a very important part in our life.

be based on ~「～に基づいている」
　Is this movie based on a true story?

Exercise A

次の日本語 (A) に相当する英単語 [句] を (B) より選び結びつけなさい。

(A)	(B)
1. 教育	1. reason
2. 改革	2. part
3. 受身の	3. result
4. 能動的な	4. admission
5. 創造的な	5. reform
6. 口頭の	6. education
7. 入学	7. oral
8. 結果	8. active
9. 理由	9. passive
10. 役割	10. creative

Exercise B

次の文章の空所を埋めるのに適切な単語 [句] を A, B より選びなさい。

1. 私たちの大学の今度の総長をどう思いますか。

   ＿＿＿＿＿＿＿＿＿ of the new president of our university?

   (A. How do you think   B. What do you think)

2. もう少し大きい声で答えなさい。よく聞こえないので。

   Please answer in a little louder voice. I can't ＿＿＿＿＿＿＿ you.

   (A. hear   B. listen to)

3. その教室にはほとんど生徒はいませんでした。

   There were ＿＿＿＿＿＿＿ students in the classroom.

   (A. a few   B. few)

4. 彼はこの国の教育改革で指導的な役割を果たしている。

   He ＿＿＿＿＿＿＿＿ in educational reform in this country.

   (A. is playing a leading part   B. is taking a leading part)

5. 学歴は高校以降のものをすべて書いてください。

   For your academic background, please _____ everything from high school on.　(A. write down　B. write on)

6. 意見は事実に基づいていないといけない。

   Your opinion should _____ facts.　(A. base on　B. be based on)

7. もっと詳しいことを知りたい方は入試事務所に電話してください。

   For further information, call the _____ office.
   　(A. admission　B. admissions)

Exercise C

次の和文を英語に訳しなさい。

1. 権威のあるイギリスの教育情報誌である *The Times Higher Education* が発表した2015～2016年の世界大学ランキングでは東京大学は43位で、京都大学は88位でした。
   「権威のある」authoritative　「教育情報誌」educational information magazine

2. 国際競争力が激化する中で、大学改革を断行して国際的に活躍する人材を育成することが今日日本が直面している緊急の課題の1つです。「断行する」put through　「育成する」foster

3. いくつかの日本の大学では、すべての学生に卒業までに海外で実習することを義務づけています。

4. すべての専門科目が英語で行われるよう外国人の教師を増やした大学もあります。
   　「専門科目」a specialized subject

5. 日本の大学でもようやく有能な学生を世界中から引き付け、次世代の世界のリーダーを育てようとする試みが始まっています。
   　「ようやく」at (the) long last　「有能な学生」capable students

UNIT 9
Merits & Demerits of Smartphones

スマートフォンの利点と欠点

日本のスマートフォンの契約数は 2014 年度末で 5750 万件であったが、2019 年末には 1 億 300 万件を超え、スマートフォンは携帯電話の 8 割を占めると推測されている。スマートフォンの最大の長所は、インターネットに容易にアクセスでき、またたくさんのアプリをダウンロードできるので、所有者はたとえ旅行中でも、多くの情報に接することができ、多彩なゲームや音楽や映像が楽しめることだ。一方、短所としては、スマートフォンは従来の携帯電話に比べて費用がかかる点や、その中に通常多くの個人情報や仕事に関連したデータなどが入っているために、失くしたり盗まれたときに、所有者が損害をこうむるばかりでなく他人にまで迷惑をかける危険があることなどがあげられている。また最近ではスマートフォンの過度の使用が特に子供たちの身体的や精神的な成長に悪影響を及ぼすと指摘する人も多い。

‖Warm-up‖

次の会話を聴いて空欄を埋めなさい。

Dialogue

A: I bought a smartphone yesterday. It's a very convenient device **by which** you can get a lot of **information**. (　　　　　　　), if you use a smartphone, you can easily locate the places (　　　　　　　　　) since it has a satellite-based navigation system.

B: What are other functions of a smartphone?

A: Well, you can call, play computer games, and browse full websites (　　　　　　　　　　　　) even while traveling.

B: In short, a smartphone is a dual combination of a conventional cell phone and a personal computer, isn't it? Doesn't it have any demerits?

A: **Yes**, it does. A smartphone itself is more expensive than other types of cell phones. **Besides**, a smartphone owner needs to buy accessories. Security is another source of concern. Since it contains valuable private and work-related data, a smartphone is a liability to hacking and identity fraud (   ). Some people are also deeply concerned that the excessive use of smartphones, (   ), could have a serious impact on their physical and mental development.

B: As is true with all convenient devices, a smartphone has both merits and demerits, doesn't it?

Notes:
merit「利点」/ **demerit**「欠点」/ **convenient**「便利な」/ **device**「機器」/ **locate**「〜の位置を突き止める」/ **satellite-based navigation system**「衛星をベースにした位置を特定するシステム」/ **function**「機能」/ **browse**「(情報などを) 検索する」/ **dual**「2つの」/ **combination**「組み合わせ、結合」/ **conventional**「従来の」/ **cell phone**「携帯電話」/ **expensive**「高価な」/ **accessory**「付属品」/ **security**「機密保持」/ **source of concern**「懸念材料」/ **contain**「〜が入っている」/ **liability to ~**「(被害など) 被りやすいもの」/ **hacking**「(コンピュータなどへの) 不法侵入」/ **identity fraud**「個人情報詐欺」/ **be concerned**「懸念している」/ **excessive**「過度の」/ **impact**「影響」/ **physical**「身体的」

文法上の注意

❏ 前置詞 + 関係代名詞

関係代名詞の節の中の動詞または形容詞に前置詞が付いているとき、この前置詞を関係代名詞の前に持ってくることができる。ただし関係代名詞 that の前に前置詞が来ることはない。

○ This is the condominium about which I spoke the other day.
○ This is the condominium which I spoke about the other day.
○ This is the condominium I spoke about the other day.
× This is the condominum about that I spoke the other day.

用法上の注意

❏ **information は不可算名詞**

「情報」、「荷物」、「商品」などは日本語では可算名詞として使われることもあるが、英語の information、baggage、merchandise は不可算名詞。

　○ There is a lot of information on Japan-U.S. relations in our library.
　× There are a lot of informations on Japan-U.S. relations in our library.
　○ Please load all my baggage into your car.
　× Please load all my baggages into your car.
　○ This store carries a lot of merchandise from abroad.
　× This store carries many merchandises from abroad.

❏ **日本語の「はい」、「ええ」、「うん」は英語では必ずしも Yes ではない**

"Don't you have a smartphone?（スマートフォンは持っていないんですか）
（はい、持ってません）
　　○ "No, I don't."　　× "Yes, I don't."
"Don't forget to mail my letters on your way to school."
（学校へ行く途中、手紙を投函するのを忘れないでね）
（うん、忘れない）
　　○ "No, I won't."　　× "Yes, I will."

❏ **besides と beside を混同しないように**

besides は「その上、更に加えて」で、beside は「～のそばに」の意

　○ Besides causing an accident, the driver left the scene.
　× Beside causing an accident, the driver left the scene.
　○ She sat beside me.
　× She sat besides me.

慣用表現を正しく覚えよう

in short「要約すると、要するに」
　He doesn't study or work. In short, he's lazy.

have an impact on ～「～に影響を与える」
　The outcome of the presidential election in the United States will have a great impact on Japan-U.S. relations.

as is true with ～「～について同じことが言えるように」
　As is true with her mother, Carol is both beautiful and intelligent.

Exercise A

次の日本語 (A) に相当する英単語 [句] を (B) より選び結びつけなさい。

(A)	(B)
1. 器機	1. information
2. 利点	2. security
3. 欠点	3. demerit
4. 情報	4. contain
5. 機能	5. merit
6. 機密保持	6. function
7. （位置を）突き止める	7. physical
8. （情報などを）検索する	8. locate
9. ～が入っている	9. device
10. 身体の	10. browse

Exercise B

次の文章の空所を埋めるのに適切な単語 [句] を A, B より選びなさい。

1. スマートフォンを使えばいろいろな情報を手に入れることができる。

    Using a smartphone, you can get _____.

    (A. various informations   B. various kinds of information)

2. スマートフォンがないとはじめてのレストランの位置を突き止めるのは難しい。

    Without a smartphone, it's difficult to locate a restaurant that is _____ you.   (A. new to   B. new for)

3. 要するにスマートフォンは通常の携帯電話とパソコンを結びつけたものですね。

    _____, a smartphone is a combination of a conventional cell phone and a personal computer, isn't it?   (A. For short   B. In short)

4. スマートフォンの価格は通常の携帯電話より高い。

    The price of a smartphone is (a)_____ than (b) _____.

    (a) (A. more expensive   B. higher)

    (b) (A. a conventional cell phone   B. that of a conventional cell phone)

5. スマートフォン所有者にとっては機密保持ももう１つ懸念材料です。

   Security is＿＿＿＿＿＿＿＿＿＿ for a smartphone owner.

   (A. another source of concern   B. other source of concern)

6. たくさん大事な情報が入っているので、失くしたり盗まれたりすると、スマートフォンは個人情報詐欺の被害を受けやすいものです。

   Since it (a) ＿＿＿＿＿＿＿＿＿＿ a lot of important data, a smartphone is (b) ＿＿＿＿＿＿＿＿＿＿ identity fraud.

   (a) (A. contains   B. concerns)   (b) (A. liability to   B. a liability to)

7. 全ての便利な機器と同様、スマートフォンには利点と欠点があります。

   ＿＿＿＿＿＿＿＿＿＿ all convenient devices, a smartphone has both merits and demerits.   (A. As is true to   B. As is true with)

Exercise C

次の和文を英語に訳しなさい。

1. 2014年度末に5750万件であった日本のスマートフォンの契約者数は2019年末に1億300万件を超えると推測されています。　「契約数」subscription　「1億」100 million

2. これは、スマートフォンが携帯電話全体の8割を占めることを意味します。

3. スマートフォンの最大の長所は、たくさんのアプリをダウンロードできるので、所有者は、たとえ旅行中でも、多くの情報に接することができまた多彩なゲームや音楽や映像などが楽しめることです。

4. スマートフォンは、通常、中に多くの個人情報や仕事に関連したデータなどが入っているために、失くしたり盗まれたときに、所有者は多大な被害をこうむるばかりでなく他人にも迷惑をかける危険があります。

5. 最近ではスマートフォンの過度の使用が子供たちの身体的や精神的な成長に悪影響を与えると警鐘を鳴らす人も多くいます。

UNIT 10
Japan's Feat of Space Science

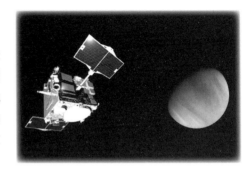

日本の宇宙科学の快挙

2015年12月金星探査機「あかつき」が金星を回る軌道に乗ることに成功した。宇宙航空研究開発機構(JAXA)によると、日本の宇宙探査機が地球以外の惑星の周囲を軌道を描いて回るのは初めてで、この探査機は金星の大気の謎を解く観測に取り組む。

「あかつき」は2010年12月エンジントラブルで金星の周回軌道に失敗したがJAXAはこの失敗に懲りず、精密な計算により姿勢制御用エンジンを開発して探査機の金星を回る軌道投入に成功した。この成功は前例のない快挙で、JAXAの宇宙科学者たちは「遂に長年の夢が実現した」と喜んでいる。

‖Warm-up‖

次の会話を聴いて空欄を埋めなさい。

Dialogue

A: I saw (　　　　　　　　　) of Venus **on TV** the other day.

B: They are ultraviolet images of the earth's nearest planetary neighbor, aren't they?

A: Yes, (　　　　　　　　) by the space probe Akatsuki (　　　　　　　　) about 72,000 kilometers from the core of Venus.

B: Didn't the (　　　　　　　) to orbit the probe around Venus result in failure **due to** engine **trouble**?

A: Yes, but by dint of precise calculations, the Japan Aerospace Exploration Agency, or JAXA, conducted an "Earth swing-by" when the probe (

) and **succeeded in switching** the probe's orbit into the gravitational pull of Venus.

B: It's amazing that space science has been **making rapid progress**. Mysteries of the universe will be solved by degrees.

Notes:
feat「快挙」/ **space science**「宇宙科学」/ **Venus**「金星」/ **ultraviolet image**「紫外線の画像」/ **planetary**「惑星の」/ **space probe**「宇宙探査機」/ **core**「中心」/ **orbit**「(天体の)軌道に乗る[乗せる]、軌道を描いて〜を回る」/ **failure**「失敗」/ **precise**「精密な」/ **calculation**「計算」/ **swing-by**「スイングバイ(軌道変更をするのに惑星の重力場を利用する飛行)」/ **gravitational pull**「引力」/ **amazing**「驚嘆すべき」/ **mystery**「謎」/ **the universe**「宇宙」

文法上の注意

❏ on TV

「テレビで」は on TV で、TV の前は無冠詞だが、「ラジオで」は on the radio と定冠詞と共に用いられる。

○ I saw the news on TV.
× I saw the news on the TV.
○ I heard the news on the radio.
× I heard the news on radio.

❏ due to

この due は形容詞で、be 動詞の後や名詞の前で使われるのは正用法だが、to を伴い because of や owing to の意味で副詞句を導くのは誤用という説があった。しかし現在では due to ... の副詞句用法は英語でも米語でも容認されている。

○ Her illness is due to stress.
○ She missed the English class today due to illness.

用法上の注意

❏ trouble と troubles

日本語になっているトラブルの感覚から trouble を複数形で使う日本人が多いが、「トラブル、故障、障害、面倒」の意味では不加算名詞である。trouble が複数形で用いられるのは「悩み事」の場合が多い。

○ I'm sorry to put you to so much trouble.
× I'm sorry to put you to so many troubles.

- ○ Pour out all your troubles to me.
- × Pour out all your trouble to me.

❏ succeed in+ 動名詞

「〜するのに成功する」は succeed in+ 動名詞で、succeed to- 不定詞は誤り。

- ○ Japan succeeded in launching an asteroid probe on Wednesday.
- × Japan succeeded to launch an asteroid probe on Wednesday.

❏ make rapid progress

不加算名詞の前に形容詞が付くと、He has a strong determination to win. の例のように不定冠詞が付くことがあるが、progress は常に無冠詞で用いられる。

- ○ Our project is making steady progress.
- × Our project is making a steady progress.

慣用表現を正しく覚えよう

result in ~「〜という結果になる、〜に帰着する」
　The railway accident resulted in the death of five passengers.
by dint of ~「〜によって」
　By dint of hard work, he passed the difficult examination.
by degrees「徐々に」
　The small boat sank beneath the waves by degrees.

Exercise A

次の日本語 (A) に相当する英単語 [句] を (B) より選び結びつけなさい。

	(A)		(B)
1.	進歩	1.	core
2.	宇宙科学	2.	mystery
3.	快挙	3.	progress
4.	宇宙探索機	4.	space probe
5.	失敗	5.	feat
6.	計算	6.	space science
7.	中心	7.	ultraviolet
8.	謎	8.	failure
9.	紫外線の	9.	planetary
10.	惑星の	10.	calculation

Exercise B

次の文章の空所を埋めるのに適切な単語 [句] を A, B より選びなさい。

1. 私はその美しい金星の紫外線の画像をテレビで見ました。

   I saw the beautiful ultraviolet images of Venus ＿＿＿＿＿＿＿＿.

   (A. on TV　B. on the TV)

2. 金星は地球に最も近い惑星です。

   Venus is Earth's nearest ＿＿＿＿＿＿＿.

   (A. plant neighbor　B. planetary neighbor)

3. 宇宙探査機を金星の軌道に乗せる最初の試みは失敗した。

   The first attempt to orbit a space probe around Venus ＿＿＿＿＿＿＿.

   (A. resulted to failure　B. resulted in failure)

4. その宇宙探査機の打ち上げはエンジントラブのために失敗した。

   The launching of the space probe failed due to ＿＿＿＿＿＿＿.

   (A. engine trouble　B. engine troubles)

5. 精密な計算によりJAXAは宇宙探査機の軌道を金星の引力に乗せるのに成功した。

(a)_____ precise calculations, JAXA succeeded (b)_____ the space probe's orbit into the gravitational pull of Venus.

 (a) (A. By dint of B. By the dint of)

 (b) (A. to switch B. in switching)

6. 日本の宇宙科学は近年急速に進歩している。

Japan's space science has recently been making _____.

 (A. a rapid progress B. rapid progress)

7. 宇宙の謎は徐々に解かれてゆくことでしょう。

Mysteries of the universe will be solved _____.

 (A. by degree B. by degrees)

Exercise C

次の和文を英語に訳しなさい。

1. 2015年12月、金星探査機「あかつき」が金星を回る軌道に乗るのに成功しました。

2. JAXAによると、日本の探査機が地球以外の惑星の周囲を軌道を描いて回るのは初めてで、この探査機は金星の大気の謎を解く観測に取り組んでいます。

3. 「あかつき」は、2010年12月、エンジントラブルで金星の周回軌道に乗るのに失敗しましたが、JAXAはこの失敗に懲りずに研究開発を続けました。

4. 精密な計算による姿勢制御用エンジンの開発が今回の成功をもたらしました。
 「姿勢制御用エンジン」attitude control engine

5. この成功は前例のない快挙で、JAXAの宇宙科学者たちは、「遂に長年の夢が実現した」と喜んでいます。 「長年の夢」a long-cherished dream

UNIT 11
Japan's Food Self-sufficiency Rate

日本の食料自給率

国の食料自給率とは、国内で消費される総ての食料のうち、国内で生産された食料が占める割合のことである。農林通産省によれば2015年度の日本の食料自給率はカロリーベースで39%であった。日本の食料自給率は6年続けて同じ数字となった。1965年度の日本の食料自給率は73%だったが、米の消費減の結果下降を続けてきた。政府は今後10年で食料自給率を45%に引き上げる計画を持っているが、この目標を達成するのは極めて困難であろう。

‖Warm-up‖

次の会話を聴いて空欄を埋めなさい。

Dialogue

A: I've **recently** read in a newspaper that Japan's food self-sufficiency rate, based on the amount of calories consumed, stood at (   ) in fiscal 2014.

B: (   ), compared with food self-sufficiency of other industrial countries, isn't it?

A: Yes, it is. The United States, (   ), has a calorie-based self-sufficiency of more than 100 percent.

B: Why does Japan depend so much on imports for food?

A: There are several factors which have **contributed to** the rapid decline in the rate **since** 1960, when it was 79 percent. One big factor is changes in the dietary **habits** of many Japanese, ( ).

B: Well, ( ) prefer **meat** and bread to **fish** and rice.

Notes:
self-sufficiency rate「自給率」／ **consume**「消費する」／ **fiscal 2014**「2014（会計）年度）」／ **industrial country**「工業国」／ **import**「輸入」／ **factor**「要因」／ **rapid decline**「急速な減少」／ **dietary habits**「食習慣」

文法上の注意

❏ recently と時制

recently は習慣的行為を表す場合は現在時制の動詞と共に用いられることがあるが、原則としては現在完了または過去と一緒に使われる。

- ○ Have you recently seen a movie?
- ○ She recently bought a new bicycle.
- ○ He used to go home once a week, but recently he goes there only once a year.
- × The number of smokers recently declines.

❏ since の正しい用法

過去のある時点の始まりを示す since が、現在まで続いている動作や状況の動詞と共に使われるときの時制は現在完了。方言では since と ago が同じ文中で用いられることがあるが標準文法では誤りとされている。

- ○ He has been in the hospital since last March.
- × He is in the hospital since last March.
- ○ He has been in the hospital for two months.
- × He has been in the hospital since two months ago.

用法上の注意

❏ habit と custom

日本語の「習慣」に相当する英語には habit と custom があるが、前者は「個人が繰り返し行うこと」なのに対し後者は「団体、地域社会または国によって行われていること」。

- ○ Many Americans have a habit of drinking coffee soon after they get up.
- × Many Americans have a custom of drinking coffee soon after they get up.
- ○ Is it Japanese custom to exchange postcards at New Year?
- × Is it a Japanese habit to exchange postcards at New Year?

❏ meat と fish

　meat も fish も種類を表すときは可算名詞として使われるが、「食肉」や「魚肉」の意味で集合的に使われるときは不加算名詞。

　　○ She's a vegetarian and doesn't eat meat.
　　× She's a vegetarian and doesn't eat meats.
　　○ Japanese used to eat lots of fish.
　　× Japanese used to eat lots of fishes.
　　○ Chicken and pork are my favorite meats.

❏ contribute to ~「~の一因になる」

　次に名詞が来る場合は問題ないが、「~する一因になる、~するのに貢献する」のようなときには、通例は動名詞を伴う。不定詞がくる構文は今日ではまれ。

　　○ Emergency imports of food from Japan contributed to helping many homeless people in that country.
　　△ Emergency imports of food from Japan contributed to help many homeless people in that country.

慣用表現を正しく覚えよう

stand at ~「(数値などが) ~である」
　The unemployment rate in March stood at 10 percent.
　ただし身長を表す場合は He stands 180 centimeters tall. のように at を入れないで用いる。

compare A with B「A を B と比較する」
　Let's compare the new dictionary with the old one.
　A と B が同じ種類のものを比較するときは with の代わりに to が用いられることもあるが、compare A to B は、Life is compared to a voyage. の文のように、「A は B に例えられる」の意でよく使われ、この意味では with は用いられない。

depend on A for B「B を A に頼る」
　She depends on her brother for her school expenses.
　「B をしてくれることを A に頼る」場合は The United States depends on Japan buying (to buy) more meat. の型をとる。

prefer A to B「B より A を好む」
　I prefer baseball to soccer.

Exercise A

次の日本語 (A) に相当する英単語［句］を (B) より選び結びつけなさい。

(A)	(B)
1. 要因	1. industrial country
2. 輸入	2. dietary habit
3. 新聞	3. consume
4. 減少	4. factor
5. 消費する	5. newspaper
6. 自給率	6. import
7. 工業国	7. decline
8. 食習慣	8. self-sufficiency rate
9. 輸出	9. rapid
10. 急速な	10. export

Exercise B

次の文章の空所を埋めるのに適切な単語［句］を A, B より選びなさい。

1. その数字は消費されたカロリーに基づいています。

   The figure ＿＿＿＿＿＿＿＿＿ the amount of calories consumed.

   (A. bases   B. is based on)

2. その国の昨年の食糧自給率は 50% でした。

   The food self-sufficiency rate of that country ＿＿＿＿＿＿＿＿ 50 percent last year.   (A. stood at   B. stood on)

3. 多くの人は喫煙は悪い習慣だと思っています。

   A large number of people regard smoking as a bad ＿＿＿＿＿＿＿＿.

   (A. custom   B. habit)

4. 本はよく友達に例えられます。

   Books are often ＿＿＿＿＿＿＿＿ friends.   (A. compared to   B. compared with)

5. 日本の食料自給率は 1965 年以降急速に減少しています。

   Japan's food self-sufficiency rate ＿＿＿＿＿＿＿＿＿ since 1965.

   (A. is rapidly declining   B. has been rapidly declining)

6. 日本人はよく生の魚を食べますか

   Do Japanese often eat raw _____? (A. fish   B. fishes)

7. 彼は未だ衣食住を両親に頼っています。

   He still _____.

   (A. depends his parents on food, clothing and shelter   B. depends on his parents for food, clothing and shelter)

Exercise C

次の和文を英語に訳しなさい。

1. 国の食料自給率とは国内で消費される全ての食料のうち、国内で生産された食料が占める割合のことです。

2. 農林通産省によれば、2015年度の日本の食料自給率はカロリーベースで39%でした。
   「農林通産省」the Ministry of Agriculture, Forestry and Fisheries

3. 日本の食料自給率は6年続けて同じ数字でした。

4. 日本の食料自給率は、1965年度以降、国内での米の消費量減の結果下降を続けています。

5. 日本政府は、食料自給率を今後10年で45%に引き上げる計画を持っていますが、この目標を達成するの極めて困難でしょう。

UNIT 12
A Low Birthrate and an Aging Society

低い出生率と老齢化社会

65歳以上の人の比率の高い社会を一般的に老齢社会と呼んでいるが、日本の社会はその典型である。現在国民の4人に1人が65歳以上で、2020年には3人に1人が65歳以上になると推測されている。生活水準の向上や医療の進歩に伴い日本人の平均寿命は2015年で女性が87.05歳、男性が80.79歳になっている。一方出生率は1970年代前半以降大幅に下がっている。日本の女性が生涯に産む子どもの平均数は1974年以降はずっと2を下回っており、2005年には1.26まで落ち込んだ。その後この数値は少しは改善されているものの2015年でもまだ1.46である。低い出生率の主な原因としては女性の高学歴化に伴う未婚化や晩婚化、子育てにかかる費用の増大、働く女性のための育児施設の不足、育児や家事労働に関する女性の負担の大きさなどがあげられている。

‖Warm-up‖

次の会話を聴いて空欄を埋めなさい。

Dialogue

A: Is it true that (　　　　　　　　　　　) in Japan is over 65?

B: Yes, it is, and the number of **elderly people** in this country is expected to **continue growing**. It is estimated that one in every three people (　　　　　　) 65 in 2050.

A: Why has the Japanese population been aging at such a fast **pace**?

B: The aging of the Japanese population has been brought about by a combination of a low birthrate and high life expectancies.

A: How low is the birthrate in Japan?
B: The birthrate in 2015 was 1.46, (   ) the 2.7 percent deemed (   ).
A: What's the major factor contributing to the low birthrate?
B: Well, many young people these days are reluctant to get married and raise families, mainly **for** economic **reasons**. **The grayer** our society becomes, **the less** (   ), and the government has taken new measures to fight the low birthrate, but its efforts have not yet borne fruit.

Notes:
birthrate「出生率」/ **aging society**「老齢社会」/ **age**「年を取る、老齢化する」/ **estimate**「推測する」/ **combination**「組み合わせ」/ **life expectancy**「推定寿命、平均余命」/ **deem**「見なす、考える」/ **maintain**「維持する」/ **factor**「要因」/ **contribute to ~**「～の一因となる」/ **reluctant**「気が進まない」/ **raise**「育てる、養う」/ **economic**「経済的な」/ **gray**「高齢化の」/ **economy**「経済」/ **government**「政府」/ **measures**「対策」

文法上の注意

❏ the + 比較級 ... , the + 比較級

この文型では、はじめの the が程度を示し、後の the がその程度だけと照応する。

The grayer our society becomes, the less the economy grows.
（私たちの社会が老齢化すればするほど経済の成長はそれだけ鈍る）

用法上の注意

❏ 「老人」に相当する英語

「老人」の直訳は old people だが、日本語でも「お年寄り」とか「高齢者」と婉曲的に言うように、英語でも一般の文章では old people を避け、elderly people とか senior citizens が使われることが多い。

❏ continue に続く準動詞

「～し続ける」と言うときは「continue+ 動名詞」も「continue+ 不定詞」も可能。
○ Please continue talking.
○ Please continue to talk.

❏ pace と結びつく前置詞

一定の速度を示す pace と結びつく前置詞は at。

○ The old man was walking at a very slow pace.
× The old man was walking by a very slow pace.
× The old man was walking in a very slow pace.

❏ reason と結びつく前置詞

「〜の理由で」と言う場合 reason に結びつく前置詞は、by reason of 〜 というフォーマルな前置詞句として使われる以外は for。

○ This elevator is not used for reasons of safety.
○ The defendant was found not guilty by reason of insanity. (formal)
× He quit his job by health reasons.

慣用表現を正しく覚えよう

bring about 〜「〜をもたらす」
　The typhoon brought about a flood in our town.
bear fruit「実を結ぶ」
　We hope your hard work will bear fruit before long.

Exercise A

次の日本語 (A) に相当する英単語 [句] を (B) より選び結びつけなさい。

(A)	(B)
1. 人口	1. birthrate
2. 出生率	2. measures
3. 生涯	3. lifetime
4. 平均余命	4. maintain
5. 維持する	5. population
6. 気が進まない	6. economy
7. 理由	7. reason
8. 経済	8. government
9. 政府	9. reluctant
10. 対策	10. life expectancy

Exercise B

次の文章の空所を埋めるのに適切な単語 [句] を A, B より選びなさい。

1. 何が急激な出生率の低下をもたらしたのですか。

    What has _____ a rapid decline in the birthrate?

    (A. brought about   B. brought down)

2. 日本の人口は急速に老齢化しています。

    The Japanese population is aging _____.

    (A. with a fast pace   B. at a fast pace)

3. 日本の低い出生率の要因となっているのは何ですか。

    What factor is _____ the low birthrate in Japan?

    (A. contributing   B. contributing to)

4. 日本の出生率は現在の人口を維持するのに必要と考えられている 2.7 よりかなり下です。

    Japan's birthrate is (a) _____ the 2.7 (b) _____ to maintain the present population.

    (a) (A. far down   B. far below)

    (b) (A. deemed necessity   B. deemed necessary)

5. 彼女は経済的な理由で結婚するのを躊躇していると言っています。

   She says she hesitates to get married ＿＿＿＿＿＿＿＿.

   (A. by economic reasons　B. for economic reasons)

6. 出生率が減れば減るほど社会はそれだけ速く老齢化します。

   (a) ＿＿＿＿＿＿＿＿ the birthrate becomes, (b) ＿＿＿＿＿＿＿＿ a society ages.

   (a) (A. The lower　B. Lower)　(b) (A. the faster　B. faster)

7. 出生率を上げようとする政府の努力はまだ実を結んでいません。

   The government's efforts to raise the birthrate ＿＿＿＿＿＿＿＿.

   (A. have not yet borne fruit　B. have not yet borne fruits)

Exercise C

次の和文を英語に訳しなさい。

1. 65歳以上の人の比率の高い社会を一般的に高齢社会と呼んでいますが、日本はその典型です。

   「典型」a typical example

2. 日本では現在国民の4人に1人が65歳以上で、2020年には3割以上の人が老齢社会の1員になると推測されています。

3. 生活水準の向上や医療の進歩に伴い、今日、日本人の平均寿命は、女性が87.06歳、男性が80.79歳になっています。

4. 一方、出生率は、1970年代前半以降大幅に下がり、日本女性が生涯に産む子どもの平均数は、2005年には1.26まで落ち込みました。

5. 日本の低い出生率の原因のひとつには女性の高学歴化に伴う未婚化や晩婚化があると言われています。

UNIT 13
Global Warming

地球温暖化

温室効果ガスの排出が原因で起こる地球温暖化は、地球の大気や海洋の平均温度が上昇する現象で、異常気象や海水面の上昇などをもたらし人類に悪影響を与えるので近年大きな問題になっている。そのため、温室効果ガスの排出量を削減するための国際機運は高まっており、2015年12月にパリで開かれた第21回国連気候変動枠組条約締約国会議(COP3)で「パリ協定」が結ばれた。この協定は、先進国だけに温室効果ガス削減を約束させていた1997年に採択された「京都議定書」とは異なり、会議に参加した196ヵ国・地域に対し、それぞれの能力に応じて温室効果ガスの排出量を削減する責任を求めている。この協定には世界の2大排出国であるアメリカと中国も関与しており、地球の平均気温の上昇を産業革命前の平均2度未満に抑える目標が盛り込まれている。

‖Warm-up‖

次の会話を聴いて空欄を埋めなさい。

Dialogue

A: In recent years, weather conditions have been abnormal (　　　　　　　　　　).

B: In some countries it rained continuously for weeks, while drought and famine dealt a heavy blow to some other countries.

A: Today, it is taken for granted that unusual **weather** is due to global warming. What's the **cause of** global warming?

B: Scientists say that (　　　　　　　　　　　　　　　　) by increasing concentrations of greenhouse gases such as carbon dioxide and methane.

Global Warming　61

A: Has the world taken any steps to control the emissions of greenhouse gases?

B: Well, (   ) to reduce greenhouse gas emissions, but chiefly because of conflicting views between developed and developing countries, no substantial progress has so far been made **in this direction**. (   ) of global warming, but they have long **insisted that** developed countries **are** wholly responsible for it and that they immediately cut the emissions of noxious gases to prevent irreversible **damage** to the environment.

Notes:
global warming「地球温暖化」/ **continuously**「連続的に、切れ目なく」/ **drought**「旱魃」/ **famine**「飢饉」/ **concentration**「集中」/ **greenhouse gas**「温室効果ガス」/ **carbon dioxide**「二酸化炭素」/ **methane**「メタン」/ **steps**「措置」/ **emission**「排出」/ **conflicting**「対立する」/ **developed country**「先進国」/ **developing country**「発展途上国」/ **substantial**「大きな、重要な」/ **progress**「前進、進展」/ **ill effect**「悪影響」/ **responsible**「責任がある」/ **immediately**「直ちに」/ **noxious**「有害な」/ **irreversible**「元に戻せない、回復不能な」/ **environment**「環境」

文法上の注意

❏ insist の使い方

米用法では insist が that 節を伴って使われるときは that 節の中の動詞は仮定法現在。

- ○ The doctor insisted that your mother go on a diet.
- ○ The doctor insisted that your mother should go on a diet.（主として英用法）
- × The doctor insisted that your mother goes on a diet.

用法上の注意

❏ weather と冠詞

weather は通例定冠詞をつけて使うが、good weather, unusual weather のように形容詞で修飾されているときや、weather permitting（天候が許せば）など特殊な例では無冠詞。現在の英語では不定冠詞を付けて使うことはない。

- ○ What's the weather like in Canada?
- × What's weather like in Canada?
- ○ We've had bad weather this year.
- × We've had a bad weather this year.
- × We've had the bad weather this year.

❏ cause of ~ と cause for ~

cause of ~ と cause for ~ を間違える人がいるが、前者は「~の原因」で、後者は「~対する理由」。

○ What was the cause of the fire last night?
× What was the cause for the fire last night?
○ I don't think he has any cause for complaint.
× I don't think he has any cause of complaint.

❏ direction と前置詞

日本語の「に」に引かれて「この方向に」を for this direction とか to this direction と誤った前置詞をつける人が多いが、正用法は in this direction。

○ I saw Professor White walking in the direction of the library.
× I saw Professor White walking for the direction of the library.
× I saw Professor White walking to the direction of the library.

❏ damage は「被害、損害」の意では不可算名詞

○ The area suffered a lot of damage from the typhoon last night.
× The area suffered many damages from the typhoon last night.

慣用表現を正しく覚えよう

deal a blow「打撃を与える」
　The big tsunami dealt a severe blow to the fishing industry.
take it for granted that ...「that 節のことを当然のこと［真実］だと思う」
　Today we take it for granted that reckless deforestation often leads to floods.
take steps「措置を講ずる、取り組む」
　The Chinese government should take immediate steps to control air pollution.

Exercise A

次の日本語 (A) に相当する英単語 [句] を (B) より選び結びつけなさい。

(A)	(B)
1. 飢饉	1. global warming
2. 回復不能な	2. environment
3. 集中	3. famine
4. 排出	4. drought
5. 先進国	5. greenhouse gas
6. 発展途上国	6. concentration
7. 旱魃	7. emission
8. 温室効果ガス	8. developing country
9. 環境	9. developed country
10. 地球温暖化	10. irreversible

Exercise B

次の文章の空所を埋めるのに適切な単語 [句] を A, B より選びなさい。

1. 異常気象は地球温暖化のせいだと至極当然のように考える人は多い。
   Many people (a)＿＿＿＿＿＿ that (b) ＿＿＿＿＿＿ is due to global warming.
   (a) (A. take for granted   B. take it for granted)
   (b) (A. unusual weather   B. the unusual weather)

2. その嵐はこの地方のりんごの収穫に大きな打撃を与えました。
   The storm has ＿＿＿＿＿＿ to the crops of apples in this region.
   (A. dealt a heavy blow   B. dealt heavy blow)

3. 水質汚濁の原因は何ですか。
   What is ＿＿＿＿＿＿ water contamination?
   (A. the cause of   B. the cause for)

4. 地球温暖化は主として二酸化炭素やメタンなどの温室効果ガスの排出が原因となっている。
   Global warming is caused mainly by the emissions of greenhouse gases such as ＿＿＿＿＿＿.
   (A. carbon dioxides and methane   B. carbon dioxide and methane)

5. 政府は放射線汚染をすぐに制御する対策を取るべきです。
   The government should ＿＿＿＿＿＿＿＿ to control radioactive pollution.
     (A. take the immediate step   B. take immediate steps)

6. 発展途上国は地球温暖化の悪影響は認識しています。
   ＿＿＿＿＿＿＿＿ recognize ill effects of global warming.
     (A. Developing countries   B. Developed countries)

7. 地球温暖化は環境に大きな損害を与えてきている。
   Global warming has been (a) ＿＿＿＿＿＿＿＿ to (b) ＿＿＿＿＿＿＿＿.
     (a) (A. doing enormous damage   B. doing enormous damages)
     (b) (A. environment   B. the environment)

Exercise C

次の和文を英語に訳しなさい。

1. 温室効果ガスの排出が原因で起こる地球温暖化は、地球表面の大気や海洋の平均気温が上昇する現象です。

2. 地球温暖化は異常気象や海水面の上昇などをもたらし人類に悪影響を与えるので近年大きな問題になっています。

3. 2015年12月にパリで開かれた第21回国連気候変動枠組条約締約国会議 (COP3) で、温室効果ガスの排出量を削減するための協定が結ばれました。
   「第21回国連気候変動枠組条約締約国会議」the 21st Conference of the Parties of the United Nations Framework Convention on Climate Change　「協定」agreement

4. この協定は、会議に参加した196ヵ国・地域に対し、それぞれの能力に応じて温室効果ガスの排出量を削減する責任を求めています。

5. この協定には、地球の平均気温の上昇を産業革命前の平均摂氏2度未満に抑える目標が盛り込まれており、世界の二大温室効果ガス排出国であるアメリカと中国も関与しています。
   「摂氏」Celsius　「排出国」emitter　「～に関与する」be party to ~

UNIT 14
A Widening Gap Between Rich and Poor

拡大する貧富の格差

世界中で貧富の差が拡大している。日本も例外ではない。日本の場合この原因の1つが雇用制度の変化にあると言われている。多くの会社は人件費を圧縮するために正規雇用を減らし、非正規雇用を増やしており、総務省の調査によると、非正規社員は全国で2千万人を超え、役員を除く全雇用者の4割近くを占めている。非正規社員は労働条件が悪く、同じ仕事をしても、賃金が正社員より通常低い。不公平な待遇に対する非正規社員の不満がいろいろな社会問題の誘引にもなっていると言われている。

‖Warm-up‖

次の会話を聴いて空欄を埋めなさい。

Dialogue

A: The gap between **rich and poor** has recently been expanding worldwide, **hasn't it**?

B: Yes, Japan is no exception. In the case of Japan, a big change in tne employment system is largely responsible for it, I think.

A: (   ) has taken place in the Japanese employment system?

B: Well, **in severe business circumstances**, (
) in Japan today place emphasis on what is called "**non-regular**" or "**non-permanent**" **employment** in place of regular or permanent employment.

A: Is it (   ) for companies to reduce their labor costs?

B: Yes, it is. Part-time or temporary workers (   ) less than full-time employees (   ).

A: **Are**n't "non-permanent workers" **dissatisfied** with their unfair working conditions?

B: Certainly they are, and it is said unfair treatment of "non-permanent" workers is leading to various social problems.

Notes:
gap「格差」／ **expand**「拡大する」／ **worldwide**「世界中で」／ **exception**「例外」／ **employment system**「雇用制度」／ **be responsible for ~**「～の」原因である／ **regular** [**permanent**] **employment**「正規雇用」／ **reduce**「減らす」／ **labor costs**「人件費」／ **temporary worker**「臨時労働者」／ **full-time employee**「正社員」／ **working conditions**「労働環境」／ **unfair**「不公平な」／ **treatment**「待遇」／ **social problem**「社会問題」

文法上の注意

❏ rich and poor

「定冠詞＋形容詞」は、「形容詞＋人々」の意味で使われるが、このユニットのdialogueのように対照的に並べられるときは定冠詞が省かれる。

○ The rich often despise the poor.
× Rich often despise poor.
○ The festival pleased both young and old.
× Young should respect old.

❏ 付加疑問

普通の付加疑問は、話し手が聞き手に自分の陳述内容に関して確認を求め、下記の例のように、主節が肯定なら否定、否定なら肯定が用いられる。

You're a student, aren't you?
He isn't married, is he?

❏ 「不満である」と be dissatisfied

日本語では自動詞でも英語では他動詞のことがる。「驚く (be surprised)」、「不満である be dissatisfied」、「怪我する (be injured)」、「満足する (be satisfied)」などがこの典型的な例である。

○ I'm satisfied with my present salary.
× I satisfy with my present salary.
○ I was suprised to hear from you all of a sudden.
× I surprised to hear from you all of a sudden.

用法上の注意

❏ in severe business circumstances

「そういう状況のもどでは」in the circumstances とも under the circumstances とも言うが、経済状態を表すときの前置詞は通例 in である。

○ Under no circumstances should you support him.
○ The refugees were living in difficult financial circumstances.
× The refugees were living under difficult financial circumstances.

❏ 「非正規雇用」は英語で？

「非正規雇用」は、日本の英文メディアでは、直訳の non-regular（または non-permanent）employment を使っているが、この語句は English speaking countries ではあまり用いられていないようなので、引用符で囲んでおくほうがよいであろう。「非正規社員」もケースバイケースで part-time worker、temporary employee, contractual worker などと訳すとよい。「派遣社員」は dispatched worker。

慣用表現を正しく覚えよう

take place「起こる、行われる」
　The game took place in Tokyo on July 1.
place emphasis on ~「~を重要視する」
　Our company places emphasis on improving working conditions.
what is called = what we [you] call「いわゆる」
　The old man lives on what is called the wrong side of the tracks.
in place of ~「~の代わりに」
　The boy attended the ceremony in place of his injured father.
lead to ~「~につながる、~を誘発する」
　The incident led to the start of civil war in that country.

Exercise A

次の日本語 (A) に相当する英単語［句］を (B) より選び結びつけなさい。

(A)	(B)
1. 待遇	1. temporary employee
2. 社会問題	2. exception
3. 格差	3. employment system
4. 例外	4. treatment
5. 労働環境	5. full-time employee
6. 雇用制度	6. social problem
7. 人件費	7. gap
8. 正社員	8. emphasis
9. 重要視	9. labor costs
10. 臨時社員	10. labor conditions

Exercise B

次の文章の空所を埋めるのに適切な単語［句］を A, B より選びなさい。

1. 日本の雇用制度に大きな変化が起きた。
   A big chance has _____ in the Japanese employment system.
   　(A. taken a place　B. taken place)

2. 非正規雇用の増加と正規雇用の減少が貧富の差拡大の原因であると言われています。
   Increased "non-permanent" employment and decreased permanent employment are said to be _____ a widening gap between rich and poor.
   　(A. responsible for　B. responsible to)

3. 貴方の会社はどうやって人件費を減らそうとしていますか。
   How is your company trying to reduce _____?
   　(A. labor cost　B. labor costs)

4. その会社は厳しい財政状態にあった。
   The company was _____.
   　(A. in difficult financial circumstances　B. under difficult financial circumstances)

5. 彼は正社員でなくて派遣社員です。

   He is not a full-time employee but a _____.

   (A. dispatched worker　B. temporary worker)

6. そのパートタイマーは労働環境に不満を持っていた。

   The part-timer _____ with his working conditions.

   (A. dissatisfied　B. was dissatisfied)

7. わが社は労働環境の改善に力を入れています。

   Our company is _____ on improving working conditions.

   (A. placing an emphasis　B. placing emphasis)

‖Exercise C‖

次の和文を英語に訳しなさい。

1. 世界中で貧富の差が拡大しており、日本も例外ではありません。

2. 日本の場合は、正規雇用を減らす代わり非正規雇用を増やすという雇用制度の大きな変化が貧富の差拡大の大きな原因だと言われています。

3. 総務省の調査によると、いわゆる非正規社員は、全国で2千万人を超え、役員を除く全雇用者の4割近くを占めています。

   「総務省」the Ministry of Internal Affairs and Communications　「役員」executive

4. 非正規社員は正社員と同じ仕事をしても、たいがい正社員より安い賃金しか払ってもらえません。

5. 不公平な待遇に対する非正規社員の不満が近年いろいろな社会問題を誘発しています。

UNIT 15
Bad Manners

マナーの悪さ

電車の優先席でお化粧をしたり、コンピューターゲームに夢中なっていてお年寄りがすぐ前に立っていても席を譲らなかったり、歩きながらメールを読んだりしている者には毎日のように出会う。日本人はマナーの良い国民とされていたが、この美徳はどこかへ消えてしまったのだろうか。家庭や学校でしっかりしたマナーを教えないためだろうか。人との直接のコミュニケーションの不足をもたらしたインターネット社会の悪い面の影響のためだろうか。殺伐とした現代の社会をもっと住みよい世界にするのにはよいマナーと他人への思いやりが大切であることを認識すべきだ。

‖Warm-up‖

次の会話を聴いて空欄を埋めなさい。

Dialogue

A: Professor Right is always complaining about the bad **manners** of students today.

B: I don't blame him. Bad manners of young people (　　　　　) are too much to tolerate. The other day I was shocked to **see schoolgirls putting** on makeup in the train.

A: I can't understand the attitude of those young people who are caught up in playing computer games on the priority seats in the train (　　　　　　　　) to elderly passengers standing before their very eyes.

B: Reading or sending e-mail messages on their smartphones while walking or

(　　　　　　　　　　　　　) is also posing a problem these days. This is not only bad manners but (　　　　　　　　　　　　　) which could lead to an accident.

A: We should realize that manners matter and good manners **help make** our society (　　　　　　　　　　).

Notes:
complain「苦情を言う、愚痴をこぼす」/ **blame**「非難する、責める」/ **attitude**「態度」/ **priority seat**「優先席」/ **elderly**「お年寄りの」/ **passenger**「乗客」/ **pose**「(問題などを) 引き起こす、もたらす」/ **behavior**「行動」/ **realize**「認識する」/ **matter**「重要である」

文法上の注意

❑「人（動物、物）が〜するのを見る（聞く）」の型

「人（動物、物）が〜するのを見る（聞く）」は「see (hear) ＋人（動物、物）＋現在分詞（原型不定詞）」の型を取る

○ I saw the little boy crossing the street.
○ I saw the little boy cross the street.
× I saw that the little boy was crossing the street.
× I saw the little boy to cross the street.

目的語の後に現在分詞が使われると「少年が通りを横切る動作の途中を見た」のであり、原型不定詞の場合は「少年が通りを横切るのをはじめから終わりまで見ていた」ことになる。

❑ help の用法

「〜するのに役立つ」は英用法では help の後は to 不定詞が原則だが、米用法では to のない不定詞が一般的である。

○ He is coming to help to fix the brakes.（英用法）
○ He is coming to help fix the brakes.（米用法）

用法上の注意

❑ manner と manners

「行儀作法、マナー」の意味では必ず manners と複数形。単数形の manner は「仕方、やり方」の意。当然のことながら manners に呼応する動詞は複数形。

○ Our parents taught us good manners.
× Our parents taught us good manner.

○ His table manners haven't improved at all.
× His table manner hasn't improved at all.
○ Ken always speaks in a friendly manner.
× Ken always speaks in friendly manners.

慣用表現を正しく覚えよう

too much to tolerate「眼に余る」
　The poor performance of that soccer player is too much to tolerate.
be caught up in ~「～に夢中になる」
　I was so caught up in reading a comic book that I forgot to call you last night.
before one's very eyes「すぐ前で」
　The accident happened before my very eyes.
　　同じ意味では right in front of someone もよく使われる。

Exercise A

次の日本語 (A) に相当する英単語［句］を (B) より選び結びつけなさい。

	(A)		(B)
1.	教授	1.	matter
2.	苦情を言う	2.	pose
3.	非難する	3.	passenger
4.	重要である	4.	priority seat
5.	態度	5.	elderly
6.	優先席	6.	attitude
7.	乗客	7.	accident
8.	お年寄りの	8.	professor
9.	もたらす	9.	complain
10.	事故	10.	blame

Exercise B

次の文章の空所を埋めるのに適切な単語 [句] を A, B より選びなさい。

1. 最近の若者のマナーの悪さは目に余る。

    Bad manners of young people these days (a)_____ (b)_____.
      (a) (A. is   B. are)   (b) (A. very much to tolerate   B. too much to tolerate)

2. 先日私は何人かの女学生が電車の優先席でお化粧をしているのを見ました。

    The other day I saw some schoolgirls _____ on the priority seats in the train.
      (A. putting on makeup   B. to put on makeup)

3. 彼らは電車の中でコンピューターゲームに夢中になっていました。

    They _____ playing computer games in the train.
      (A. were caught up in   B. caught up in)

4. お年寄りの婦人が君のすぐ前にたっていたら席を譲るべきです。

    If an elderly woman is standing (a) _____, you should give your seat to her.
      (A. before your very eye   B. before your very eyes)

5. 自転車に乗りながらスマートフォンでイーメールを読むのは大変危険です。

    It's very dangerous to read e-mail messages (a)_____ while (b) _____.
      (a) (A. by your smartphone   B. on your smartphone)
      (b) (A. getting on a bicycle   B. riding a bicycle)

6. 私たちはマナーが大切なことを認識すべきです。

    We should realize that manners _____.
      (A. matter   B. important)

7. よい礼儀作法は私たちの社会をより住みよい場所にするのに役立ちます。

    Good manners _____ our society a better place to live in.
      (A. help make   B. help making)

Exercise C

次の和文を英語に訳しなさい。

1. 先日2人の女子高校生が電車の優先席でお化粧をしているのを見ました。彼女たちはお年寄りの女性がすぐ前に立っているのに席を譲りませんでした。

2. 昨日自転車に乗りながらスマホでメールを読んでいた若者がもう少しので私にぶつかるところでした。

3. かつて日本人はマナーのよい国民とされていましたが、この美徳はどこかへ消えてしまったのでしょうか。

4. マナーの悪い若者の増加の原因のひとつとして、インターネット社会で人との直接のコミュニケーションが不足していることが挙げられています。

5. 私たちの社会をもっと住みよい場所にするのには、良いマナーと他人へのおもいやりが大切であることを学ぶべきです。

COLLOCATION EXERCISES

　英語を勉強している人々は最近「コロケーション」という言葉を見たり聞いたりすることが多くなったと思いますが、「コロケーション」とは何のことでしょう。

　「コロケーション」は、ある単語がほかの単語と一緒に用いられること、また一緒に用いられる語と語の組み合わせのことです。

　幼い頃から海外で育ち英語で生活をして来た人を除いて、日本人が英語を書いたり話したりするときは、まず日本語で考えて、その日本語に相当するような英語を見つけるのが普通です。このとき一番苦労するのがこの「コロケーション」、特に動詞と名詞の結びつきです。

　日本語は便利で、名詞に「する」を付けて簡単に動詞が作れますが、英語ではどうでしょうか。日本語の「する」に一番近い英語の"do"をつければほとんどの動詞は作れますか？

　確かに「宿題をする」は"do one's homework"と言えますが、「昼寝をする」を"do a nap"、「成功する」を"do success"と言うことはできず、それぞれ"take a nap"、"achieve [win] success"としなければいけません。日本語で、「将棋」は「指す」のに対し「碁」は「打つ」と言って、「将棋を打つ」、「碁を指す」としないように、英語にも単語と単語の間には特別な「相性」があるのです。そこで、本テキストの補遺として、「動詞＋名詞」のコロケーション問題を載せておきましたのでやってみてください。日本語では動詞表現を使う場合でも英語では「動詞＋名詞」が活用されることが多いので、今後英語らしい英語を書いたり話したりするときに必ず役立ちます。

Supplementary exercises

次の各文の文尾の動詞より正しいものを選び空所を補いなさい。

1. 彼は学校へ行く途中で事故に遭いました。

　　He _____ an accident on his way to school. (had, met)

2. 昼休みを利用して私は宿題を終えた。

　　I _____ an advantage of the lunch break to finish my homework.
　　(made, took)

3. 彼女はためらわずに私の忠告を聞き入れた。

　　She _____ my advice without hesitation. (received, took)

4. 私は精神的支援をしてくれるよう級友に訴えた。

   I _____ an appeal to my classmates for moral support. (asked, made)

5. 生徒全員が校長の話に耳を傾けた。

   All the students _____ attention to the principle. (paid, took)

＊＊＊＊＊＊

6. 私はたいがい寝る前にお風呂に入ります。

   I usually _____ a bath before I go to bed. (enter, take)

7. 目的を達成するために全力を尽くしなさい。

   You should _____ your best to achieve your goal. (do, make)

8. 妹は昨夜かわいい女の子を出産した。

   My sister _____ birth to a cute bay girl last night. (gave, made)

9. 学校当局は非行少年少女対策で知恵を絞っている。

   School authorities are _____ their brains trying to devise steps to cope with delinquent boys and girls. (racking, working)

10. 大学を卒業したら一緒に商売しよう。

    Let's _____ business together after we graduate from college. (do, carry)

＊＊＊＊＊＊

11. サンフランシスコに電話をしたいのですが。

    I'd like to _____ a call to San Francisco. (give, make)

12. 雨の日の運転には十分気をつけなさい。

    _____ great caution when you drive a car on a rainy day. (Give, Use)

13. いちかばちかやってみろよ。優勝するかもしれないぞ。

    _____ a chance. You may win first place. (Make, Take)

14. そこに原子力発電所を建てる前に環境問題を真剣に考慮すべきです。

    We should _____ serious consideration to the environmental problems before building a nuclear power plant there. (give, take)

15. 太平洋をヨットで単独横断するのには勇気が要ります。

    It _____ courage to sail across the Pacific solo in a yacht. (gets, takes)

Collocation exercises

16. 台風は稲作に大きな損害を与えました。

    The typhoon _____ heavy damage to the rice crops. (did, gave)

17. かろうじて締め切り時間に間に合った。

    I barely _____ the deadline. (made, got)

18. その件については決断を下す前によく考えてみなさい。

    Think twice before you _____ a decision on the matter. (give, make)

19. 国内生産だけではわれわれの需要を全て満たすことはできません。

    Domestic production alone cannot _____ all our demands. (meet, provide)

20. この単語の意味が分からなければ、辞書で調べなさい。

    If you don't know the meaning of this word, _____ a dictionary.
       (consult, look)

* * * * * *

21. 今夜はあなたがお皿を洗う番よ。

    It's your turn to _____ the dishes this evening. (clean, do)

22. 昨夜とても恐ろしい夢を見ました。

    I _____ a terrible dream last night. (had, saw)

23. 彼女は英語の試験に合格しようとできるかぎりの努力を尽くしています。

    She is _____ every possible effort to pass the English exam.
       (making, putting)

24. アメリカでは4年ごとに大統領選挙が行われます。

    In the United States they _____ a presidential election every four years.
       (carry, hold)

* * * * * *

25. 弟は来年大学入試を受けます。

    My brother will _____ a college entrance exam next year. (receive, take)

26. 彼女の赤いセーターが私の目に留まった。

    Her red sweater _____ my eye. (caught, took)

27. 勘定を払うよう五郎に言うと、彼は嫌な顔をした。

    Goro _____ a face when I told him to pay the bill. (gave, pulled)

28. 岡教授の最終講義が終わると、私たちは教授に拍手を送った。

　　We _____ Professor Oka a big hand when his final lecture ended. (gave, sent)

29. 妻に、私の財布を見なかったかと尋ねたところ、彼女は首を振った。

　　When I asked my wife if she had seen my wallet, she _____ her head. (shook, swang)

30. 彼女の突然の死を知ったジョンは悲しみに打ちひしがれた。

　　Her sudden death _____ John's heart. (beat, broke)

******

31. 叔父は私によい仕事が見つかるよう尽力してくれた。

　　My uncle _____ his influence to find me a good job. (did, used)

32. 彼は最近サッカーに興味を持ったようだ。

　　It seems that he has recently _____ an interest in soccer. (caught, taken)

33. 先生は時々冗談を言って生徒を笑わせた。

　　The teacher _____ jokes now and then and made the students laugh. (cracked, gave)

34. あなたは日本の地図がかけますか。

　　Can you _____ a map of Japan? (draw, write)

35. 年を取ったものだ。妻の誕生日を忘れてしまうんだから。

　　I'm getting old. The date of my wife's birthday _____ my mind. (passed, slipped)

******

36. 彼女は落第させられたのでスミス先生の悪口を言った。

　　She _____ Mr. Smith names because he flunked her. (called, told)

37. 少年はハンカチで鼻をかんだ。

　　The boy _____ his nose on a handkerchief. (blew, rubbed)

38. 木はわれわれの生活の中で重要な役割を果たしています。

　　Wood _____ an important part in our life. (acts, plays)

39. 将軍はクーデターで政権を握った。

    The general _____ power in a coup d'etat. (caught, took)

40. 彼は旅行中毎日何を食べたかを記録していた。

    He _____ a record of what he ate every day during his trip. (kept, made)

※ ※ ※ ※ ※ ※

41. クリスマスに七面鳥を食べる習慣はいつアメリカに根付いたのですか。

    When did the custom of eating turkey at Christmas _____ root in the United States? (keep, take)

42. 両親は私を大学にやるのにいろいろ犠牲を払いました。

    My parents _____ sacrifices to send me to college. (made, paid)

43. 君の言うことは支離滅裂だ。

    What you say doesn't _____ sense. (make, mean)

44. 彼は私たちの大学のためにいろいろ尽くしてくれた。

    He has _____ many services for our university. (done, made)

45. 僕らが口論をすると、父はいつでも妹の肩を持つ。

    Our father always _____ sides with my sister when we quarrel. (gives, takes)

※ ※ ※ ※ ※ ※

46. バスは直線道路に入るとスピードを上げた。

    The bus _____ speed when it reached the straight road. (gathered, raised)

47. 私たちは暇つぶしによくトランプをしたものだった。

    We often played cards to _____ time. (kill, lose)

48. 監督の作戦を批判したい気持ちは分かるが、今日のところはぐっこらえて黙っていろ．

    I know you want to criticize the manager's strategy, but you'd better _____ your tongue today. (hold, kept)

49. 私は商用で来月中国へ行きます。

    I'll _____ a business visit to China next month. (go, pay)

50. 両親の意見は私にとって重要です。

    My parents' opinions _____ weight with me. (carry, put)

80   Collocation exercises

Writing Contemporary Topics in 15 Units
文法・用法もよくわかる トピック英作文15章

編著者	木 塚 晴 夫
発行者	山 口 隆 史

発 行 所　㈱音羽書房鶴見書店

〒113-0033　東京都文京区本郷 3-26-13
TEL 03-3814-0491
FAX 03-3814-9250
URL: http://www.otowatsurumi.com

2017年 3 月 1 日　初版発行
2022年 4 月10日　3 刷発行

組版　ほんのしろ
装丁　吉成美佐（オセロ）
印刷・製本　㈱シナノ
■ 落丁・乱丁本はお取り替えいたします。

EC-065